Chag Sameach

Open this book and let the pages inside
inspire a smile
ignite Jewish pride
teach a lesson or two
enlight and discover
take it all in - from cover to cover.
As you enjoy the Chag from beginning to end
And spend time with family and friends
Remember your Oorah family who cares
And will keep in touch throughout the whole year.

- Rabbi Chaim Mintz

732-730-1000 · OORAH.ORG · THEZONE.ORG · TORAHMATES.ORG · JEWISHLITTLESTAR.ORG

Life SUPPORT

Stories of
MY CHAPLAINCY AND BIKUR CHOLIM ROUNDS

RACHEL STEIN

ISRAEL BOOKSHOP
Publications

Life
SUPPORT

Stories of
MY CHAPLAINCY AND
BIKUR CHOLIM ROUNDS

RACHEL STEIN

Book design by: Rivkah Lewis

Published by:
Israel Bookshop Publications
501 Prospect Street
Lakewood, NJ 08701

Tel: (732) 901-3009
Fax: (732) 901-4012
www.israelbookshoppublications.com
info@israelbookshoppublications.com

Printed in the USA

Distributed in **Israel** by:
Shanky's
Petach Tikva 16
Jerusalem
972-2-538-6936

Distributed in **Australia** by:
Gold's Book and Gift Company
3- 13 William Street
Balaclava 3183
613-9527-8775

Distributed in **Europe** by:
Lehmanns
Unit E Viking Industrial Park
Rolling Mill Road,
Jarrow, Tyne & Wear NE32 3DP
44-191-406-0842

Distributed in **South Africa** by:
Kollel Bookshop
Ivy Common
107 William Road, Norwood
Johannesburg 2192
27-11-728-1822

ACKNOWLEDGMENTS

ODCHA HASHEM
ELOKAI B'CHOL LEVAVI...

*W*ITH LOVE AND appreciation to my supportive husband and children, for allowing Bikur Cholim to be part of our lives.

To Michele Asa...how would I or Bikur Cholim survive without you? Working together has strengthened our friendship and made it that much more rich and beautiful. For all of your support, love, and endless giving, for sharing laughter and tears and everything in between...I have no words. Just pages and pages in my heart.

To Chavie Spotts, Bikur Cholim's staunch and loyal third leg. You have given and continue to give in your quiet, unassuming way, and we treasure partnering with you. When you moved to

Atlanta, the value of our neighborhood increased exponentially. Thank you for being you, dear partner and friend. You are a gem!

To Jennifer Yaffee. With each mile we've journeyed together, our friendship has grown ever richer. Thank you for the laughter, the closeness, and everything else I've gained from you.

To Mrs. Malkie Gendelman, whose skilled editorial pen tweaked, clarified, and enhanced every page of this book. Thank you for your endless patience and devotion to this project. What a privilege to work with you!

Heroes
OF TODAY

Who are the heroes of today?
Those we admire,
Those who inspire us to reach higher,
Paragons of strength complete their marathons,
Emerging victorious
Over unimaginable trials,
With grateful yet humble smiles.
Goals that seem monumental,
Impossible tasks,
Beyond our finite grasp—
They accomplish,
With extraordinary ability,
And we marvel at their agility.

Victims of disease
Fight for survival,
Enduring untold trials,
Endowed with the realization
Of the preciousness of time,
That each moment is a sign
To exult in life.
Shimmering diamonds
Exuding rare, exquisite beauty…
We gaze in admiration,
Approach with awe and trepidation,
Hoping to learn successful navigation,
For this journey called life.

PART 1
INTRODUCTION

EMORIES OF CLOSED doors and hushed conversations float through my mind like wisps of clouds in a hazy sky. I am a three-year-old girl with long, brown hair and hazel eyes, and my father lies dying in his room. By the time I am four, he is gone, a victim of lung cancer—at thirty-five years of age.

Did I block out memories of the seemingly gentle, handsome man whom I only know through pictures, or was I really too young to hold onto these memories? One memory does stand out in my mind—so tangibly, in fact, that I can almost reach out and touch it, but I wonder: am I really remembering this scene, or have I relived it so many times that it just feels real to me?

It's a memory of myself as a little girl still in a crib. Perhaps since I was her baby, my mother kept me in a crib for a long time. In this specific scene, I daringly lift one foot over the bar and then the other. Before I know what is happening, I am sprawled in a heap on the floor, sobbing piteously. In runs my strong Daddy. He quickly scoops me up and holds me tightly over his big, strong shoulder, and I snuggle into his warmth.

Growing up, I didn't miss the man who left me fatherless, simply because I couldn't remember him. Still, I missed *having* a father and a home that was complete and normal. Any time teachers directed us to "tell your parents" something, I cringed. Father's Day was a time to mourn. My mother was a young, struggling widow who never recovered from losing her husband. My father had been her lifeline, pulling her from a difficult childhood and walking her to happiness and security. And then, a mere nine years after their marriage, he had left her anchorless.

Not surprisingly, I was a serious, sensitive child. From a very young age, I found myself gravitating toward elderly people. Perhaps because I also didn't have grandparents, I found the elderly to be cute, fun people who twinkled when they laughed and exuded unconditional love. I loved visiting elderly neighbors and residents in the nursing home. I formed relationships with these people, and savored the satisfaction of a good visit with them.

I was also driven to help people who were sick, and I pumped my youthful energy toward that endeavor. At age fourteen, I volunteered in a cancer hospital, drawing immense satisfaction from bringing sunshine into the patients' days.

I married when I was only eighteen. Hashem gave me special *siyata d'Shmaya* in finding my *bashert*, and I eagerly set about building a home together with him—a solid, rich home that, I hoped and prayed, would stand on the sturdy legs of two parents.

During the first ten years of our marriage, we lived in five different cities. In each city, I always made it my business to ferret out lonely, elderly people and "adopt" them as "grandparents." My children were always able to elicit smiles and delighted exclamations from these people, and we could never stay long enough at their residences.

When I was twenty-five and surrounded by a brood of young children, my mother was diagnosed with acute myopic leukemia, the disease that would take her life in only fifteen months. It was the first time in my married years that we lived only a two-hour drive from my mother's home in Philadelphia, and I hoped to take advantage of this fact and visit my mother as often as possible. However, I was expecting at the time, and in my state, the "only two-hour drive" proved to be too much for me to handle alone. But I couldn't expect my husband to drive me each time; besides for his own busy schedule and responsibilities—he was the *rav* of the Jewish community where we lived—I needed him to hold down the fort and take care of the children while I was away. I was in a quandary about what to do.

Then, a very special friend of mine named Elaine made me an astoundingly beautiful offer one day. "I'll help you with this, Rachel," she said. "My kids are all in school now. It's amazing—I never thought I'd see the day, but it actually does happen! So I'm free and available to drive you to visit your mother. I'll take along a book or a needlepoint, and I'll sit in the hall during the visit. You stay as long as you want. It will be my pleasure."

"I can't ask you for such a favor," I protested. "It's too much."

"Rachel, I wouldn't have offered if it were too much. It's my pleasure, really. Let me help, please. What day do you want to go?"

Reluctant though exceedingly grateful, I acquiesced, and the next day we were on our way.

Elaine and I did this every week for about a month. We were

there with my mother on the day that her *neshamah* left this earth and soared Heavenward.

After the *shivah*, I approached Elaine and tried to put my deep gratitude into words. "How can I ever thank you?" I asked her through a haze of tears. "How can I ever repay you for what you did for me?"

Elaine lovingly put her hand on my shoulder. "This is what I want you to do. When someone needs help, *you* be there for *them*. And that is how you will repay me."

Elaine smiled her gentle smile, and I felt like I was looking at an angel. Perhaps I was. I nodded, but didn't really find her answer satisfying. Until years passed, and I moved to Atlanta, Georgia, where I co-founded a *bikur cholim* organization that was to eventually grow into a central pillar in my life. And every once in a while when, through my *bikur cholim* activities, I'm *zocheh* to help someone in some small capacity, I think of Elaine. I figuratively lift a cup to my special mentor and friend, and tell her, *Elaine, this one's for you.*

PART 2

"HELLO, G-D, IT'S ME, DAN MILLER, REPORTING FOR SERVICE."

ASHEM BLESSED ME and my husband many times over with healthy children. Life became extremely busy on the home front, but with good things. While I was in the midst of raising my growing brood, a young man in our community was diagnosed with cancer. His name was Danny Miller, and he was to become the impetus for our *bikur cholim* organization.

I remember calling my dear friend Michele Asa and telling her in a trembling voice, "Did you hear? Danny Miller has cancer again."

A sharp intake of breath greeted my words, and we cried together as we held the receivers. Danny was in his thirties, and he and his wife, Elaine, had a young child. Danny had had several bouts with cancer, and though he would go into remission after each one, the cancer kept returning with a vengeance.

That was when I felt a rush of determination. *No!* I told myself. It won't happen! There won't be another young widow left alone to fend for herself, or a vulnerable little orphan tossed anchorless into the stream of life. *Hashem,* I cried, *what do You want from us? We'll do anything! Just please, I beg You, spare Danny Miller's life. Let him walk his son, together with Elaine, into adulthood.*

Michele and I asked Danny if we could create a *bikur cholim* organization as a *zechus* for his recovery, as there was no organized *bikur cholim* establishment in the community at the time. Danny agreed, and that was how our Bikur Cholim was born.

Were Danny's years extended, even though he only lived until age thirty-nine? The doctors called him a medical miracle who should never have survived his fourteen battles with sarcomas. Yet survive he did, beyond all medical predictions, with his infectious smile and happy-go-lucky attitude that made everyone who knew him treasure this man's pure essence.

"Hello, G-d. It's me, Dan Miller, reporting for service." This sign hung in Danny's bedroom, where he saw it first thing in the morning every day. He was a true soldier in Hashem's army, learning and living a life of Torah with every fiber of his being. He was actively involved in supporting our city's day school long before he was blessed with a child of his own.

After one of his many bouts with cancer (his first was when he was fourteen), his leg was amputated, and he was fitted with a leg prosthesis. One friend reported going to visit Danny following this harrowing surgery. Nervous and unsure what to expect, never having seen an amputee before, Saul entered the room.

Danny lit up when he saw his visitor.

"Want to see my stump?" he exclaimed jovially, whipping

away his blankets and showing off his bandaged stump, flopping it around in a comical manner.

When he walked out of the room, Saul dissolved into tears, not for Danny, but for everyone else in the world who is blessed with health and a lot more, yet who still feels discontent. *If only such people could meet Danny*, he thought, wiping his eyes.

Saul had a brother who was diagnosed and hospitalized with Hodgkin's lymphoma. When Danny heard about it, though he himself was dreadfully sick, he asked if he could swing by Saul's brother's room to cheer up the patient.

Danny had the power to make you feel like you were his best friend in the world, and that nothing mattered more to him than his friendship with you. His way of smiling when he spoke, his insightful way of looking into people's eyes and seeming to peer into their souls…

⎯⎮⧵⎮⧵⎮⧵⎮⧵♡⎯

Mr. B. was an eighty-year-old man who had grown up fatherless during the Great Depression and fought as a soldier in Europe during World War II. An independent and "self-made" individual, he remained active and loved life, until diabetes ravaged his body, requiring him to undergo a leg amputation. The surgery didn't only rob him of his leg; it robbed him of his self-reliance, too, which was devastating for Mr. B. He couldn't get out of bed by himself, use the bathroom, drive, or do any of the activities that made his life meaningful.

Danny heard about the situation. Taking time for an elderly man whom he had never met, Danny showed up at Mr. B.'s rehab facility, determined to cheer up a downtrodden soul. Unfortunately, Mr. B. was in therapy when Danny arrived.

Danny left him a warm note and several magazines with articles about people who had lost a limb, and then left. From that day on, Mr. B. began to push himself to use his artificial titanium leg. With renewed spirit, he taught himself how to maneuver his body in and out of his wheelchair and bed without assistance.

Without ever meeting Mr. B. face to face, Danny had left his mark on him.

He was an ardent follower of Aharon Hakohen, a person who cared about and vibrantly loved everyone…

⎍⎍⎍♡

THE MIDDLE OF a busy highway is not the ideal place for a car to overheat—especially a car filled with young children. But since my husband had never laid down the rules for his hitherto trustworthy Ford, that's exactly what it did, and it began to spew forth billows of smoke.

Cruising along this same highway, on their way to a family party, Danny and Elaine Miller caught sight of our predicament. They immediately stopped their car and insisted on waiting with us until help arrived. No matter that their plans were halted. No matter that Danny was sick. They saw a need—and responded with love.

⎍⎍⎍♡

HE LOVED CHILDREN with a passion, aligning himself with their innocence and pure delight in the business of living. He took great pleasure in playing with the neighborhood kids, and sometimes entertained them with his fake leg; he would take it off and swing it like a baseball bat or twirl it baton-style, leaving the children doubled over with laughter all over his lawn.

Once, the third-grade class of our local day school sent him get-well cards. Danny went to school in a wheelchair and thanked the class. He then called each child individually to express his appreciation.

His voice was deep and rich, and I remember calling him after one of his surgeries.

"How are you?" I asked, afraid to hear the answer.

"I'm great, and how are you?"

Did I hear right? Was this man for real, asking how *I* was the day after his major surgery? The *malach hamaves* certainly was no match for such a force, I was sure.

⎯⎯⎯⎯⎯

DANNY WAS A true friend, the kind Hallmark cards write about. Every person who crossed his path was treated to his shining smile. Even the Terminex exterminator who serviced much of our community wanted to visit Danny during his frequent hospitalizations!

One beloved friend, Yaakov, recounted the following poignant story. It was a bitterly cold, snowy night in January, a night when most people stayed huddled inside their heated homes. Yaakov and his family lived on a steep hill. On that icy night, Yaakov heard a knock on his door. He opened the door, and his mouth fell open. A flickering candle lit up the darkness. There was Danny, holding a cupcake with a glowing candle, wearing his trademark grin.

"Happy birthday, old buddy," Danny sang.

⎯⎯⎯⎯⎯

DANNY'S LAST DAYS were punctuated by breathing difficulties. His breathing would stop and start, again and again. He said he wouldn't give up without a fight; he loved life too much to just let go.

While in hospice for a day of attempts at pain management, Danny suddenly asked for his son, Elan.

"Where's Elan?" he cried out. "I want to do his homework with him."

He was in such pain and on such heavy drugs. Yet he struggled to keep his eyes open in order to help Elan with his homework.

"I care about Elaine; I want to do more for her. Soon I won't be able to. How will she manage?" Danny confided his worries to his close friend Yaakov during those pain-filled, worrisome hours in the hospice center, leaving Yaakov to marvel at Danny's angelic selflessness.

WHILE ENDURING RIGOROUS chemotherapy, Danny would find other Jewish patients in need of some cheer. Wheeling himself into their rooms, Danny Miller performed *bikur cholim*.

Torah rejuvenated him. His eyes lit up when a new thought was presented. He arranged to be *chavrusos* with several people in the community, determined to master as much Torah as he could. When his condition prevented him from attending shul, he would ask friends to repeat the rabbi's *drashah* so he wouldn't miss out on it. Even when lying on his hospice bed, aware that his days were numbered, he asked his visitors to say *divrei Torah*. During those moments of Torah exchange, Dan's pain was alleviated.

When his situation looked bleak, Danny's rabbi advised him to have a name added.

"But I like the names I already have," Danny protested with a smile.

His already lengthy name, Shaul Chanoch Nachum Zelig ben Barbara Ellen, was on all of our lips, as we prayed constantly for his recovery.

"Just add Chaim," his rabbi told him.

Some close friends made a party in honor of Danny and his new name. Shouts of "*L'chaim*, Chaim!" rang out as Danny's friends toasted him, hoping that maybe the harsh decree would be changed together with his name. Dan beamed at them all, reveling in his friends' love, and radiating hope and sunlight.

IT WAS DUE to our community's unanimous love for this cherished man who was so sick, that my friend Michele and I took the great leap of opening our *bikur cholim* organization. We launched it with a grand kick-off event, featuring Rebbetzin Chana Weinberg *a"h* as our honored keynote speaker.

Weak but determined, Danny attended the event, too. He spoke following Rebbetzin Weinberg's presentation, limping toward the podium to give a *dvar Torah*. He concluded his words with a pitch asking people to get involved in this new initiative. Our tears flowed, and our audience gave him a standing ovation as he returned to his seat.

Three committees were introduced under our *bikur cholim* banner: visits to hospital patients, visits to nursing home residents, and visits to those who are homebound. Event attendees were invited to sign up for whichever committee they felt they could join.

Over time, the organization expanded to taking school

groups to nursing homes on a monthly basis, hosting a "Mommy and Me" program in nursing homes, having a medical equipment *gemach*, and providing meals and transportation for medical needs.

Danny tried to stay involved and endeavored to make us into a non-profit organization. But his sun was setting, and one day I got a call.

"Rachel?" his devoted wife said softly. "We're asking the community to come over today. Danny wants to say goodbye."

I nodded into the phone, unable to speak. How could we do this?

The Millers' house resembled a shul during the Yamim Nora'im. Throngs of people stepped forward to tell Danny how he had impacted their lives and the lives of their children. We quietly stood in line, waiting our turn to stand in front of our friend and role model. After guaranteeing him, "We'll never forget you, we promise," we went into another room to speak on a video. The video, which also contained a private message from Danny to his beloved wife and son, would be presented to Elan upon his bar mitzvah—so that he would know the stuff his father was made of and how much the community loved him.

At one point, Danny's eyes closed. He was tired, and his medication made him drowsy.

"Danny?" said his wife.

Suddenly Danny's eyes opened wide, and he roused himself. With holy strength, he roared, "I'm not dead yet! I can still *daven* Minchah to Hashem!"

Immediately, a *minyan* many times over formed around him, and our community experienced a second Yom Kippur, a day that will be forever engraved in the hearts of all who were there.

Several days later, Danny's pure *neshamah* ascended to his

Father and King. As a fitting tribute, our *bikur cholim* organization decided to dedicate all of its efforts *l'ilui nishmaso*.

Our community compiled a book of memories and presented it to Elaine upon Danny's *shloshim*. I penned and included the following letter:

Danny, on the day of your levayah, *I came home emotionally laden and drained. It occurred to me that a visit to the nursing home would be a fitting tribute to your memory, as a continuation of the* bikur cholim *organization established in your merit.*

I loaded up my children, myself, and a friend into my van and began driving to the nursing home. We had almost arrived at our destination when I was suddenly struck by a realization: my twelve-year-old son was due home any minute, and he didn't have a key! Picturing him standing outside an empty house in the dark led me to turn around the car, step on the accelerator, and race back home, all the while glancing around nervously for flashing blue lights.

I rushed to unlock the door, and exhaled in relief when my son smiled at me from inside the house; he had entered through an unlocked side door. Relief, though, soon changed to concern.

"Yaakov, do you smell gas?"

"I have a cold, Mommy. I can't smell a thing."

Tracing the fumes to the kitchen, I discovered a gas burner on—minus the flame. The vapors were overwhelming.

I immediately connected the dots, realizing that my negligence in not giving my son a key, for which I had berated myself while zooming home, had actually turned out to be a gift from Hashem. My Yaakov was safe.

Did you intercede on his behalf, Danny? Your presence felt so real, so tangible. Thank you, Danny, for being a meilitz yosher *for my Yaakov.*

When we subsequently returned to the nursing home, our elderly friend Rachel *was thrilled to see us.*

"Moishele!" she called out exuberantly to my four-year-old, extending a trembling hand to him. "Moishele, come here."

My little son's eyes sparkled as he approached her and made her evening.

This mitzvah was for you, Danny.

L'chaim, *Chaim!*

PART 3
ONCE UPON A BIKUR CHOLIM

E HAVE TO give ourselves a name," Michele told me one day. "We can't just call it 'our *bikur cholim* organization.'"

And so, we thought of the name "N'shei Chessed," and that's the name we gave our organization…that is, until someone came along and poured a bucket of ice water on it.

"Rachel?" the caller asked me. "Did you really name your organization N'shei Chessed?" His voice was incredulous.

"Yes," I answered innocently.

"How could you?" he ranted. "To name it after the break-off shul, those double-crossers who deserted us and caused such conflict in the community. What were you thinking?! It's a terrible thing!"

This was the first time I understood what it meant to be steamrolled.

"Scratch 'N'shei Chessed,'" I informed Michele, filling her in on the call.

When my husband heard about the call, he assured me that our organization would be a success. "Anything worthy of an attack from the *yetzer hara*, just as it's sprouting above ground, has got to be a good thing," he insisted.

Comforted, Michele and I simply embraced the title "Bikur Cholim of Atlanta," or "Bikur Cholim" for short.

And we went right on with our *bikur cholim* activities.

A PASTRAMI SANDWICH ON RYE

"RACHEL? JERRY SCHOEN is in the hospital and needs visitors." It was our shul secretary on the line.

"How long has he been there?" I asked.

"Two weeks," she replied.

"Two weeks?!" I exclaimed.

Jerry Schoen was an older man who was still learning the fine nuances of *Yiddishkeit*. But he was a proud and very active member of the shul's men's club, and our committee had actually met with him recently to brainstorm together for ideas on how to improve Bikur Cholim. And now here he was, in the hospital himself, for two weeks, no less—with no visitors! I grabbed my pocketbook and ran, arriving just as he was being wheeled into an ambulance to be taken to a rehab facility.

"Hello, Mr. Schoen!" I greeted him, falling into step alongside his stretcher. "How are you? I'm so sorry I didn't know you were here until now."

"It's good to see you." He smiled his one-hundred-watt smile. Then he reached for my hand—and I panicked. I guess he'd forgotten about the "no touching women" rules.

"Here!" I said without thinking, offering my pocketbook strap in lieu of my hand. "Take this instead."

Immediately, I bit my lip, wondering if my instinctive response had embarrassed him. I pictured my mitzvah sailing out of reach, like a balloon floating up to the clouds.

A few days later, I sat with Jerry Schoen in his room in the facility, trying to assess his needs.

"I'm sorry I reached for your hand," he said, his blue eyes twinkling. "I forgot."

"And I'm sorry I gave you my pocketbook strap to hold! That wasn't such a nice gesture," I answered, and we both laughed heartily.

I set up Jerry with regular, daily visitors who would bring him supper when they came. Mothers came with young children, and he always greeted them warmly. Visiting with Jerry was such an uplifting experience that people wanted to come back.

One day, Jerry told me that a young mother from the community, Mrs. Young, had just visited him with her little daughter. The girl had promptly sat down on the floor and drawn a picture for Jerry, while the mother asked him if there was anything he might need that she could get for him.

"I would love a pastrami sandwich on rye," Jerry boomed, a wide grin on his lips and a gleam in his eyes. "With all the fixings: mustard, mayo, ketchup, you name it. And tomatoes, onions, and pickles, too. Ah, well," he sighed wistfully, "maybe when I get out of here..."

The next day, Jerry told me, in marched Mrs. Young again— with not one pastrami sandwich in hand, but two! "I thought I had died and gone to Heaven," he finished his story with a laugh.

A SOUTHERN BELLE

THERE WAS NO one like Mrs. B. She was a unique, Southern-born Jewish woman who showered everyone with love, laughter, and requests for rides home from the supermarket. Sometimes we ducked when we saw her ambling down the aisle, because you couldn't rush Mrs. B. She didn't understand racing to appointments and carpools. But she certainly understood warmth and love.

She'd endured infinite hardships: she lost her husband at age fifty, and each of their three children had either a physical or mental disability. Yet somehow, she greeted every day and every person with a smile. Mrs. B. embraced our community like we were her extended family; our *simchos* were hers, and she toasted our joyous occasions with her ever-present mug of coffee mixed with pareve creamer.

Toward the end of her life, Mrs. B. was stricken with late-stage cancer. Sadly, there was little the doctors could do for her, and week by week, she steadily declined. During her last days, Mrs. B. was not aware of her surroundings. She spoke gibberish to her many close friends who came to say goodbye. When I came to her bedside, her eyes flew open.

"How y'all doin', Rachel?" she asked, totally lucid for that moment.

I grasped her hand and gave her a big kiss. "It's wonderful to see you, Mrs. B. How are you doing?" I asked, fighting to keep my smile bright and my tears at bay until I left the house. *Do you have to go, Mrs. B.?* my heart cried out in protest. *Can't you stay with us forever?*

At her *levayah*, the rabbi said that she was the only woman who got away with giving him orders. She used her energy and personality to arrange a women's Shabbos *shiur* for nineteen years. And she used to pull out roller skates to dance with at weddings.

Some people know how to make the world a more colorful place.

～～～♡

WHEN ANGELS DANCE

TRUNDLING ALONG IN my geriatric but still viable, wintergreen, fifteen-seater van, I followed the line of teachers' vehicles as we made our way to the nursing home. One of Bikur Cholim's programs involved bringing middle school students to nursing homes or assisted living homes on a monthly basis. Watching the students interact with these elderly residents was other-worldly.

On this particular occasion, an eighth-grade girls' class had just put on a performance for the residents. Once their performance was finished, the girls continued singing—and suddenly, a few girls broke out of their line formation, taking the hands of those in wheelchairs and swaying back and forth with them. Other girls formed a circle and danced around the room, and the residents who were able to dance joined in. It was a spontaneous dance—but it was the dance of the century. I can still close my eyes and see the exquisite beauty of the scene, the smiles of the girls as they locked eyes with their elderly friends. A fire was ignited in the hearts of many lonely souls on that day.

～～～♡

DOES SHE KNOW I'M HERE?

Every Friday my children and I trekked to the nursing home to wish the Jewish residents a good Shabbos. But there were times I wanted to skip Ruth's room.

Ruth was seemingly paralyzed in body and soul. Every week I found her in the same position, lying sideways on her bed, her face turned to the wall. Sometimes her eyes were closed and she seemed to be sleeping; other times she stared vacantly straight ahead.

"How are you, Ruth?" I would say as I bustled in, putting a wide smile on my face.

"Oh, what beautiful flowers!" I exclaimed one week.

"You have adorable grandchildren," I told her another time, admiring the pictures on her wall. *But where was her family, those smiling, full-of-life faces beaming from those pictures? Were they too busy to come and visit their ailing mother and grandmother?*

"How are you feeling, Ruth?" My question would dangle like a spider on a gossamer string. There was never any answer to it.

Sometimes Ruth would emit a low moan, and I wondered if she were in pain. I would take her gnarled hand and stroke it gently. In slow motion, she would occasionally turn her head, focusing her large, liquid brown eyes on me.

"It's okay," I would soothe, wanting it to be. "It's okay."

Was that a ghost of a smile or a grimace on her face?

"She seems uncomfortable," I once told a nurse.

"Okay, I'll be in," she assured me. And she went right back to eating her lunch.

Does my visit really make a difference? I wondered. *Does Ruth even know I'm here?* Yet an invisible force prodded me to pop in week after week. Until one week, I peered into her room and her bed was empty. My heart dropped, and I knew.

I stopped a nurse. "Ruth?" I asked, the word quivering with poignancy.

"Expired," she said. "I'm sorry."

Yeah, me, too…I'll miss her. A wave of sadness washed over me. It took me a minute to absorb the nurse's callous comment, and in a volcanic instant, my lava erupted within me. *Expired?! Was that how the nurse saw Ruth? What did she think Ruth was—a bag of lettuce turned brown, past the recommended due date on the package?!* But the nurse had already passed me by.

At least your suffering is over, Ruth, I thought with a deep sigh. *I won't forget you.*

The wheels of time spun forward, and years passed. Fridays were no longer designated for nursing home visits, as my family was *baruch Hashem* growing and more needy of my time and attention, especially on Erev Shabbos.

I had one child who struggled with various issues. I *davened* for him; I hoped; I cried. He so desperately needed his own personal *yeshuah.*

"Where are you going, sweetie?" I asked one day, noticing that he kept looking out the window.

"Someone's taking me to the game," he tossed over his shoulder.

"Who?" I wanted to know.

"Ben," my son said. "I forgot his last name."

I know Ben. He goes to our shul. I wondered how he had come to connect with my son.

"So nice!" I replied, grateful and bemused. Distracted, I reached for the ringing phone.

"Mrs. Stein?" a man's deep voice greeted me.

"Yes?"

"Ben Caplan here. Can you tell your son I'll be there in about five minutes?"

"Sure, thank you." My heart hammered inside of me. Was it a rush of hope? "This is so nice of you."

"No problem. He's a nice kid. And I don't know if I ever thanked you for visiting my mother all those Fridays."

"Your mother?" I echoed.

"Yeah. Remember Ruth?"

THE CALL OF THE SHOFAR

It was Erev Yom Kippur when my friend Meira and I set out to visit Chana, a single elderly woman who was in a rehab facility, recovering from a broken leg. We thought we were giving of ourselves by going to cheer a lonely soul. To our surprise, we received a priceless gift from her in return.

"I have a story for you," Chana said to us after we'd pulled chairs over next to her wheelchair. "I finally understand now why I had to go through this whole situation of a broken leg and having to be in rehab."

Wow, I thought. *That's pretty impressive.* I leaned forward, my curiosity piqued.

"On the first day of Rosh Hashanah," Chana began, "Rabbi G. came by to blow the shofar for me. We closed the door so the noise wouldn't bother any of the other residents—most of the others here aren't Jewish. Just when the rabbi lifted the shofar to his lips, a knock sounded on my door.

"'Come in,' I said, and Rabbi G. and I waited.

"'Hi,' a middle-aged woman said. 'I'm with my father next door, and I noticed you holding a shofar. Would you mind coming to his room and blowing for him, also?'

"'With pleasure,' Rabbi G. replied.

"'Two for the price of one,' I quipped. I didn't even know they were Jewish.

"I wheeled myself into the room next door. Moments later, we were all gathered around the woman's father's bed, and Rabbi G. said the *brachah* and lifted the shofar. A mighty blast filled the room, and I tried to focus my thoughts properly. And then it happened. The elderly man in the bed whispered, '*Tekiyah.*'

"His daughter gasped. After Rabbi G. had finished blowing the shofar for us, we left the room, and the daughter followed us into the hallway.

"'I want you to know,' she said, 'that ever since my father's stroke five months ago, he hasn't been able to speak. That *tekiyah* that he said was his first word. The shofar must have really sparked something in his soul. I can't thank you enough.'

"So you see," Chana concluded, her blue eyes dancing with delight, "this must be the reason Hashem put me here—so that a Jewish soul could be kindled and united with Hashem at this all-important time of year. Isn't that terrific?"

"Chana," Meira said, putting a hand on her shoulder, "*you're* terrific. You should have a *refuah sheleimah b'karov*, and a *gemar chasimah tovah.*"

We left with tears in our eyes. That elderly man's *neshamah* was not the only one kindled by the clarion call of the shofar.

BACK TO THE LIVING

Awe-filled silence filled the shul as we caught our breath, riveted by the sight of Baruch Sugarman approaching the *bimah*. In a voice choked with emotion, he fervently *bentched Gomel*, and we, his friends and community, wiped our glistening eyes and answered with a resounding, "Amen." From March second until March nineteenth, Baruch ben Sara Raizel, now Chaim Baruch ben Sara Raizel, was mentioned in each of our heartrending *tefillos* and daily Tehillim gatherings. Devoted husband, father of several small children, and a serious *ben Torah*, Baruch almost succumbed to a life-threatening illness. In a breathtaking vision of astounding *hashguchuh*, accompanied by worldwide love and support, Baruch recovered and merited to return to the loving embrace of his family, friends, and community.

Baruch had tested positive for the flu on Friday, and by Monday he was still feeling severely unwell. Concerned, he and his wife, Leah, returned to the doctor. The doctor ordered some x-rays, and pneumonia showed up on them. Baruch was told to go to the hospital for what they assumed would be a day or two. They would later find out that the pneumonia was caused by Group A Strep bacteria, which made it a much more serious strain of pneumonia.

"Please go home and get my *tallis* and *tefillin*," Baruch said to Leah, and they agreed that she would bring them along when she came to the hospital later, after doing carpool and tending to the children.

A few hours later, Baruch called Leah, telling her that they were talking about intubation. The couple struggled to understand what was happening and how Baruch's condition had deteriorated so rapidly.

"Can we try to avoid that?" Baruch asked the nurses.

They tried an oxygen mask, but his breathing continued to worsen. *I'm doing better*, Baruch scrawled hopefully on his white board and showed it to the nurse. *No need to intubate*. But the medical staff didn't buy it, frightened as they watched his rapid downward spiral.

Within hours of being admitted to the hospital, Baruch was put on a ventilator. As he continued to decline, it was determined that he was in septic shock and his kidneys were failing. Within twenty-four hours, he developed cardiogenic shock (where the heart can't pump enough blood for the body's needs) and cardiomyopathy (disease of heart muscle in which the muscle is abnormally enlarged, thickened, or stiffened). His heart was functioning at 20 percent of its normal capacity. That Tuesday, the cardiologist motioned to Leah to follow him out of the room.

"I need to talk to you," he said, his expression grave. "You have to realize that your husband is very sick. Probably the sickest person in the entire hospital right now. It's time to call in your family and your rabbi."

In a daze, Leah started making calls, alerting Baruch's mother, family, and their rabbis and intimate friends.

On Tuesday night, Leah was introduced to the infectious disease doctor, who explained the terrible aggression of strep pneumonia. It had spread throughout Baruch's body with breakneck speed. "The next forty-eight hours are critical," the doctor pronounced.

With tears in their eyes, Leah and a close friend of Baruch's discussed where Baruch would want to be buried if the unthinkable happened. Baruch's friend, who was also a rabbi, approached Baruch's bedside and said *vidui*.

In spite of this, Leah erroneously thought that her husband still had a 50 percent chance of recovery; in reality, though, his chances were much lower than that. Still, not having a full understanding of Baruch's dire situation helped give Leah hope and strength to get through the next grueling few days, until his situation did indeed begin to turn.

Baruch's condition quickly degenerated. The infection was

causing multi-organ failure, and the medical staff struggled to keep his blood pressure at 80/40. At one point, Baruch had twelve active medicines dripping into him in order to stabilize his heart, blood pressure, and the infection. The doctors had to paralyze Baruch and put him into a drug-induced coma to control his breathing on an oscillator (they couldn't even use a ventilator anymore due to the precariousness of his condition).

While their lives hung in abeyance in the hospital ICU, Hashem sent many candles to illuminate the Sugarmans' darkness. A doctor who was a close friend, Dr. S., stepped in to help, with incredible devotion, throughout Baruch's illness. After a full day of work, or sometimes during a lunch break, she would come to the hospital, monitor Baruch's situation, and explain the intricacies of his condition in layman's terms to the family, so they could understand. Her unstinting support meant a lot to the Sugarmans.

Family and siblings, both local and those who flew in, took over the Sugarmans' household, ensuring that the children would have as normal a routine at home as was possible, while close friends took hospital shifts. Meanwhile, our entire community, galvanized into action, responded with an unprecedented outpouring of love and concern. *Rabbanim* and friends proved to be an incredible source of strength and support to the family, giving time and energy through visits, encouragement, and their caring. The *rav* of the community left in the middle of an important meeting as soon as he heard what was going on, driving immediately to the hospital to be with Baruch and his family. Thereafter, he continued to provide emotional support to the Sugarmans. Women's nightly Tehillim recitations were organized. Additionally, many of us took on to say daily *perakim* of Tehillim so that the entire *sefer* would be said each day in Baruch Sugarman's *zechus*.

Bikur Cholim took charge of sending meals to the family. To our amazement, almost no phone calls were necessary in order to organize the rotation. So many people wanted to help that the schedule was filled weeks in advance! People took on *kabbalos*, desperate to add *zechusim* to the Heavenly account so that Baruch would live.

On Wednesday, Ta'anis Esther, Leah was hit with the news that Baruch's liver was failing. But that was also the first day that they saw some baby steps forward, as tests showed that Baruch's kidneys were improving. This was a big thing, and Leah began clinging to a gossamer string of hope.

Still, Baruch wasn't out of the woods yet—far from it. There was a real fear that his heart and liver had sustained permanent damage. We, as a community, felt a black cloud suspended over us. How could we enjoy Purim while the Sugarmans were facing life and death?

"*Hakadosh Baruch Hu* wants us to be *mesamei'ach* on Purim," the *rosh kollel* announced on Purim night. "We should joyfully perform all of the *mitzvos hayom*, and may it be a *zechus* for Baruch's *refuah*, as well as for the other *cholim* in the community." A few chapters of Tehillim were said before Megillah reading, and Purim arrived in Atlanta, with heartfelt prayers interspersed throughout the day, as we tried to smile and carry on with our obligations.

Leah wanted the kids to enjoy Purim. With superhuman strength, and fueled with the knowledge that Baruch would also want them to be happy, she took her children to hear the Megillah, to deliver *mishloach manos*, and even to a fun-filled Purim *seudah*. Back in Baruch's hospital room, a friend came in, clad in full Persian garb, from floral vest to roomy pants tucked into his socks, and *leined* the Megillah, bringing the spirit of Purim into the hospital room and into the Sugarmans' hearts; when Leah heard about it, it gave a tremendous boost to her spirits.

We witnessed the light and power of Purim, a day of answered *tefillos* and *yeshuos*. From that day on, Baruch only improved; there were no major setbacks. Commensurate with the breathtaking speed of his sudden decline was his upward climb toward health. We watched and listened, astounded, as he defied doctors' predictions from one day to the next.

As each day passed, Leah would go home and try not to show her tears. "Tatty's getting better," she assured her children. "He just needs some help with his breathing."

"We miss Tatty. Will he be home for Pesach?" the children asked.

"*B'ezras Hashem.* Your Tatty loves and misses you very much and is fighting hard to be able to come home," replied Leah.

For the most part, the Sugarman children remained calm throughout the storm that held everyone in its grip. They knew their *tatty* was sick, but they were confident that he would get better. After all, they were *davening* for him together with their teachers and friends! Malka, who was in kindergarten, made sure her class said Tehillim each day for her father. Moshe, the Sugarmans' four-year-old son, helped his *morah* make cookies to send to the nursing staff. And all the kids sent Baruch colorful get-well cards.

Their oldest daughter, Shira, recorded videos of herself and her siblings for their father to hear. Leah would play them for Baruch, with the hope that hearing the children's voices would elicit a positive reaction.

"Why do you have to go back to the hospital?" Shira asked her mother one day.

"Because Tatty needs me," Leah replied.

"I know Tatty needs you," Shira told Leah, her eyes streaming.

"But I need you, too. I wish you could be with Tatty and with me, also."

So do I, my child, so do I, Leah thought to herself. And she wrapped her daughter in a warm hug.

At one point, Leah asked the doctors what to expect if Baruch were to pull through.

"In the best-case scenario," a doctor explained, "he'll probably be in the ICU for a few weeks on the ventilator, progressing to a regular room for a period, and then he'll be moved to a rehab facility to relearn how to do everything. It can take six months to a year for Baruch to regain full physical strength."

That Friday, a dear friend of Leah's flew in from Florida to spend Shabbos with her in the hospital. As the two women were driving to the hospital, Leah's doctor-friend, Dr. S., called with a positive update about Baruch's condition.

"Leah," she said, "this is the first day I feel I can breathe."

Together Leah and her friend from Florida *bentched licht,* and it was very peaceful; they went into Shabbos with a good feeling.

Shortly afterward, the infectious disease doctor came in to see Baruch. "I think he's going to pull through this," she told Leah.

Baruch continued to hold his own. On Shabbos day, the cardiologist came in and told them that he liked what he saw on the echocardiogram that day and that he did not believe Baruch's heart would sustain any permanent damage.

On the following Monday, one week from the day he went into the hospital, Baruch was switched from the oscillator back to the ventilator. Various tests and blood work continued to show improvement, and there was talk of possibly extubating him later that week.

Late Tuesday afternoon, Leah received a call from one of the nurses. "We are going to start waking Baruch up and plan to extubate him today. We will then monitor him overnight to see how he does."

Leah could not believe what she was hearing. *Could it really be?* she wondered, feeling like she was living in a dream.

Twenty-four hours later, a speech therapist came to see Baruch in the ICU, to determine what he would be able to eat. The expectation was clear liquids only. But Baruch passed his swallow test with flying colors, resulting in the therapist clearing him for all foods immediately.

"I remember when I was only allowed to have a wet sponge touch my lips," Baruch says. "Then I graduated to ice chips, and then water. What a gift it was to be able to drink water!"

That same day, a physical therapist came to assess Baruch's capabilities. To the therapist's amazement, he was able to stand and take one step with the assistance of two people holding him. Baruch was kept under observation for two more nights in the ICU, and by Thursday he was moved to a regular room. Within a few days, he was able to walk a few hundred feet with a walker and was practicing going up a stair.

The doctors and nurses were amazed at how quickly things were turning around. Baruch's organs were all rebounding, and it didn't look as though there would be any long-term damage. They said he was a "save" and a miracle.

By Monday of the following week, they were talking about discharge, but wanted to do a stress test first. "For a healthy person, a stress test requires walking or running on a treadmill," Baruch explains. "But because I was so weak and could not do that, they had to inject a nuclear drug instead, in order to check how my heart was functioning. It made me feel horrible—hot, nauseous, and sick. It was during this test that the realization of what I had been through hit me. It was the first time I broke down and cried. Later that afternoon, after reviewing the results of the test, the cardiologist recommended that I undergo a heart catheterization to check for any blockages; he was afraid I might have one, as the bottom of my heart didn't seem to be functioning properly under stress."

Distraught, Baruch called his *rosh kollel*. "I was so close to coming home," Baruch told him, "and now this came up!"

With pithy wisdom, the *rosh kollel* gave over a powerful lesson in *bitachon*. "Baruch," he said, "what part of your recovery process have the doctors gotten right?"

"Nothing," Baruch admitted.

"So what are you worried about?" the *rosh kollel* concluded, and Baruch could feel his warm smile touching him through the phone.

The heart catheterization was set up for that Thursday morning.

"Your arteries are perfectly clear," the cardiologist informed him afterward. It was an awesome day. Baruch was discharged that afternoon.

"How could a quiet person like me elicit such an overwhelming response, among so many people?" Baruch wonders, having been filled in about what went on around him while he was in the hospital. "As soon as I took sick, I had thousands of people *davening* for me; people kept passing my name around. Leah's sister, who lives in New York, said a co-worker with no connection to us saw my name on the bulletin board in her shul. Old friends I grew up with, people who are not even *frum*, were *davening* for me every day. The news of my illness traveled to Eretz Yisrael, Texas, New York, New Jersey..."

"Wait, you know the Sugarmans, too?" some of Baruch and Leah's friends asked people who forwarded the texts and postings with Baruch's name.

"No, but this looks important," came the reply, and people continued to pass around the name and picture of the husband and father of young children, with a plea to *daven* for him.

Responding to Baruch's query, his rabbi remarked, "When a meteor crashes in your neighbor's backyard, you take notice."

"When people see me now, they get very emotional," Baruch says, shaking his head with wonder at all that has taken place. "They saw me in the hospital, so sick and incapacitated. They can hardly believe that I'm up and functioning now, *baruch Hashem*.

"There are so many lessons from this," Baruch concludes, his luminous eyes providing a window into his pure *neshamah*. "Everything happened so suddenly. I didn't have a chance to say goodbye to my wife or children, to spend time with them. And now Hashem gave me my life back! I can't be the same person I was before. What a responsibility I now have! After a hundred and twenty years, I want to tell Hashem that I made good on His investment in me."

One person—a whole world. *Baruch Rofei cholim.*

After experiencing this story together, our community seems closer, gifted with a renewed understanding of the preciousness of every breath of life.

―♡―

STANDING AT THE CROSSROADS

YESTERDAY, ON A Thursday afternoon, my husband and I went to visit our former neighbor and friend, a ninety-two-year-old widower who recently moved out of his home of fifty years and into an assisted living facility. During weekly phone calls, he mentioned how much he missed the shul, and we could hear wistful notes of loneliness in his voice. The smile that lit up his eyes when we came to visit him stayed with me for the rest of the day.

Brimming with energy and wit that belied his age, Mr. G. proudly introduced us to his new friends while taking us on a tour of the beautiful facility. He extolled the activities offered in the facility—the amenities; the caring, friendly residents and personnel; and his spacious and immaculate apartment there—but still, an undercurrent of sadness laced his words.

"There's just one thing I don't understand," he finally said. "Why can't we have an assisted living facility right in the neighborhood, instead of so far away from the community? There's such a need…"

"I wish I knew," I agreed, meeting his gaze. "I know many people have dreamed and tried to create something like that, but for whatever reason, there were always roadblocks in their way. It's very painful to have to move away from your community and your shul."

"Yes," Mr. G. said, looking away. "My children come to see me whenever they can, and I can't tell them how I feel. I have to be happy and cheerful, so I don't bring them down. But it's hard."

We nodded. "They have their own lives," he continued. "And I don't want to burden them."

I pointed to an album on Mr. G.'s table. "Can I see this?" I asked.

"Of course," he said.

Celebrating Mr. G. and his now-deceased wife's sixty years of marriage, the album featured an impressive compilation of pictures and beautiful letters from their children and grandchildren.

"You have a beautiful family," I said softly, after turning the last page.

"Yes, I do…" A smile played on Mr. G.'s lips, but that unmistakable sadness radiated from his eyes. "You made my day," he told us when he walked us out. "Thank you so much for coming."

Just a few hours after that poignant visit, I got a phone call that set my heart on fire.

"My wife is in labor," Mr. Tepper told me, "and it looks like we'll be in the hospital for Shabbos. Are you able to organize food for us? Would it be too much trouble?"

"In labor?" I squealed, tears blurring my vision. "*B'sha'ah tovah!* I'm so happy for you."

"Yes, *baruch Hashem.* We've been married seven years, you know," he said, and I heard the wonder in his voice. "Seven and a half years, actually."

Wow, I thought. Every week in their marriage that passed with no news was surely fraught with pain. Seven years indeed. And a half.

"It would be my pleasure to arrange food for you," I replied. "Will you let me know when you have good news?"

We exchanged numbers and then hung up, and I set about coordinating Shabbos food. With a prayer in my heart, I eagerly anticipated the special call while going through my day. On Friday morning, I woke up to a text showing Mr. and Mrs. Tepper cradling their beautiful daughter, and my eyes spilled over as I happily showed the picture to my husband and some friends. When I came to the hospital toting Shabbos food for the new parents, I gave them a heartfelt *brachah* and marveled over their adorable baby girl.

You be good to your parents, I silently told the baby as I held her, awed by her miraculous existence. *They went through so much until you came.*

Mr. Tepper showed me her little t-shirt with the words "I was worth the wait" on the front. His eyes shone with joy; no words were necessary.

Driving home, I couldn't help but contrast these two episodes of *bikur cholim* in which I was involved, one right after the other. The first concerned what would probably be a significant last step on a lifetime's journey—a lonely and painful last step, much as Mr. G. tried to make the best of it. The other concerned the first step of a brand-new life; it was a step that sparkled with promise and unknown potential.

And I found myself *davening* for the people standing at both of the crossroads...

LET ALL OF MY BONES PRAISE HASHEM...

ONE YEAR, MY fellow committee heads Michele and Chavie (the third indispensable leg of our committee, who does so much, yet remains inconspicuously behind the curtains) decided to tackle another angle of *bikur cholim,* and they organized a bone marrow drive, under the auspices of the Jay Feinberg Gift of Life Foundation.

The Gift of Life is one of the nation's public bone marrow and blood stem cell registries, located in Boca Raton, Florida. Jay Feinberg, founder and CEO of the Gift of Life, was diagnosed with leukemia in 1991. He was told that he would need a bone marrow transplant to survive, but the doctors' predictions were grim; they didn't think he had a chance of finding a matching donor, since Jay was Jewish, and a patient's best chance of finding a match lies with those of similar ethnicity.

Jay's family and friends launched a huge campaign, enabling people to be tested and registered to give bone marrow. This result-ed in tens of thousands of new donors in the worldwide registry. Four years of these bone marrow drives passed, yet no match was found for Jay. Finally, a man decided to organize one last drive; his best friend had found a match through a drive organized for Jay, and he was determined to reciprocate the kindness to Jay. In May of 1995, the last donor tested at this last drive…and he turned out to be Jay's match. Jay received his transplant soon after, and he has devoted his life to helping other sick people find the matches they so badly need, too.

Besides the Jay Feinberg Gift of Life Foundation, other organizations are also involved in this great mitzvah. In Eretz Yisrael a number of years ago, *bachurim* from Yeshivas Toras Moshe thronged to be tested for a bone marrow drive organized by Ezer Mitziyon. The father of one of their friends was sick and in desperate need of a transplant. So many boys turned out that the people doing the testing ran out of tubes! Unfortunately, no match was found for this boy's father. Yet the wheels of *hashgachah* were turning…

Two years passed, and then one day, an unsuspecting *bachur* from Yeshivas Toras Moshe received a startling call that he was a match for a child battling leukemia. Without reservation, he underwent the procedure whereby some of his bone marrow was transferred to the child. Thousands of miles away from his home and his family, this *bachur* was hospitalized so that he could save a life.

Although it was an outpatient procedure, it took the boy two weeks to fully recover and be able to get in and out of his bunk bed without pain. With trademark humility, he didn't talk much about the great deed he performed. His story only became salient to me when Hashem joined his destiny together with our family's, and he married our daughter. Now, every year during Chanukah, our son-in-law, daughter, and their little girl attend a *seudas hoda'ah* made by the family of the boy whose life our son-in-law saved. It is there that they are able to see firsthand the gift of life that they helped perpetuate.

PART 4
VALIANT VOLUNTEERS

HE IS JUST IRREPLACEABLE

*A*N OLDER MAN, Mel needed help getting to shul on Shabbos. This entailed wheeling him down his very steep, long driveway, shadowing him in shul, and then wheeling him back up his "mountain" to get home. With Hashem's help, I found the perfect volunteer for Mel—a kindhearted man named Baruch Weissman.

Two years passed. I forgot about that situation as I moved on to others. Until Mr. Weissman called me up one day.

"I just wanted to tell you that we're expecting a baby any day," he said. "My wife really needs my help, and I think I'm going to have to pass on this mitzvah of volunteering for now. I'll help you find a replacement."

But finding a replacement that made Diane, Mel's wife, happy was not easy. Many volunteers were dismissed after their first attempt at the job.

"Rachel," Diane told me, "you have no idea what Baruch Weissman did for us all these years. He was like a son to Mel. Not only did he take him to shul, he stood next to him the entire time and helped him keep the place. When Mel needed the bathroom, he took him. When shul was over, he wheeled Mel to the shul's kiddush and waited for him to finish there before wheeling him home. He is simply just irreplaceable."

"Oh," I said, awed by my young volunteer's dedication and *tzidkus*. I didn't know. I didn't know that ordinary people can climb such lofty summits and do the extraordinary... But I was learning.

JUST AN ORDINARY GUY

"RACHEL, MY BOARDER has a medical condition that is flaring up. He needs to be driven to an appointment that is six hours away. Is that something you can help him with?"

"Hmm, let me see what I can do and I'll call you back."

I thought of Mark Berger, an unemployed man whose heart definitely exceeded his limited bank account, and I called him to ask if he'd be available to do this *chessed*.

"Well, I have an appointment that morning... You know what? Let me call you back in a few minutes."

In less than five minutes, Mr. Berger called me and said he had rescheduled his appointment and would be happy to drive the young man to his doctor's visit.

"Mr. Berger," I said, "that's amazing. I want to pay you for your time. You're giving up your entire day, plus gas, to do this *chessed*. Please keep a *cheshbon* and let me know how many hours you spend on this."

"Okay," he said.

On the day of the doctor's appointment, I waited to hear from Mark. When he didn't call me, I called him.

"How did it go?" I asked.

"Oh, it was great," he answered. "We *chazered hilchos Sukkos* together the whole time, which is wonderful because Sukkos is just around the corner. I learned so much—it was great!"

"I'm so glad." I smiled into the phone. "So how many hours was it? I'd like to write you a check."

"Listen, Mrs. Stein," Mark said, and his voice took on a firm tone. "It was twelve hours of my time. I want you to calculate the amount you were going to give me and put it right back into Bikur Cholim's account, so it can help someone else. And… thanks for the opportunity."

I stood there dumbly, holding the phone long after our connection had been severed. This guy had no job, and a wife and baby to support. Was he for real? An ordinary man, no different from you or me. Doing extraordinary things.

TWO MEN ON A MISSION

IT WAS A Thursday afternoon, Bikur Cholim had been relatively quiet that week, and Shabbos preparations were the biggest thing on my mind. Until I opened my email, and a note with an urgent request appeared in my Inbox, making my insides tighten with tension. Would we be able to fill the request? I wasn't sure. Our pool of volunteers was small at the time, and I racked my brain for ideas of who would be available and willing to step up to the plate as I quickly reread the note.

Good morning:

I am writing to you from Massachusetts, in reference to the son of one of our senior volunteers. Mr. Yisrael Azani's son, Shalom Azani, is currently hospitalized in Atlanta, in Northside Hospital. He had open-heart surgery there this past week.

Mr. Azani came to his volunteer job this morning crying and very upset. He was reluctant to burden anyone with what happened, but when we pressed him, he told us about his son's surgery and how concerned he is about his son being in a hospital so far away. He has another son, Dovid, who accompanied Shalom to Atlanta for the surgery, but Mr. Azani is still concerned, as neither Dovid nor Shalom know anyone in the Jewish community there.

We would like to find out if there is an active *bikur cholim* team that could keep an eye out, so to speak, for the son, Shalom Azani, and his brother, Dovid. It would give Mr. Azani a bit of relief to know that his children are not alone.

Thank you,
Ariella Baruch, LMSW
Tov V'chessed Bikur Cholim

With a *tefillah* in my heart, I forwarded the email to six men that came to mind. In minutes, a note appeared from Yossi, one of my newer volunteers:

I can go now to visit the son, he assured me.

Amazing! I wrote back. *Thank you.* Tizkeh l'mitzvos, *and please let me know what happens.*

A few minutes later I received a note from Moshe, another volunteer, telling me that though he was presently out of town, he would be back by Friday and available to help out then. *Do they need Shabbos food?* he wanted to know. *I can be the courier.*

With emails flying back and forth through cyberspace, and my potato kugel and chocolate cake made in between, we finalized plans. I connected Yossi with Moshe, and the two decided to team up and deliver Shabbos food together to the Azani brothers the next day.

Within an hour, Shalom and Dovid received a wonderful visit from Yossi. And the story continued on Friday.

I prepared a bulging laundry basket with food for two, and slipped in some *Mishpacha* magazines, challah, grape juice, and an electric candelabra. At twelve o'clock sharp, a car pulled up in front of my house, and my phone rang.

"You're here?" I asked.

"Yup," came my volunteers' response.

"I'll be right out."

Stepping out of his car to take the laundry basket from my hands, Yossi's eyes glowed, and his smile stretched from ear to ear. Moshe sat in the passenger seat wearing a matching smile, and my heart contracted.

Two total strangers unexpectedly dropped into our lives, and these men had put everything aside in an effort to lighten their darkness. Of course, no Jew is a stranger, but still...

I marveled at how these special men were able to fit into a regular-sized car with their oversized hearts. I found my eyes watering as I followed their car's trail until it turned my corner, and a sense of *nachas* pervaded my being. *I'm proud of you, guys,*

I thought, feeling a surprising sense of motherly connection to these two grown men. Two men on a mission.

Slowly, feeling uplifted by these angels in human form, I walked back into my kitchen to spice my chicken.

$$\rightsquigarrow\heartsuit$$

THE PERK LADY

WHEN ANSWERING A call, I often scroll through my mental Rolodex and ask Hashem to help me find the right volunteer. The truth is, *all* of my volunteers never fail to amaze me, with their level of dedication, willingness, and self-sacrifice.

"How did you become involved in the mitzvah of *bikur cholim*?" I ask Deena K. one day. Deena is a veteran volunteer who's been with us since our inception. The real question dangling beneath my words is: how do you do it? How do you visit people almost every day of the week, always prepared with your ready smile and an endless supply of patience, caring, and warmth?

Deena flashes me the smile that has cheered countless people over the years and replies with the following story:

"Many years ago, before there was an organized *bikur cholim* group in our community, Edith, a woman with terminal cancer, called our rabbi to ask for assistance. She was totally alone, without any relatives to help her out, and in her state, she really needed help. The rabbi presented the situation to the shul, and a shul member with a golden heart offered to take Edith into her home.

"Many of us took turns visiting Edith and bringing her food. I was not from the big-time cooks, so I simply brought myself and gave her the only commodity I had to offer—my time. Sadly, her situation deteriorated quickly, and within a few weeks, she was admitted to a hospice facility.

"One day when I visited her in hospice, she made a comment that I struggled to decipher. With difficulty, she repeated her words: 'Ah, here comes the Perk Lady.'

"She must have seen the puzzled look on my face, because she explained what she meant. 'When you come to see me, your visits perk me up.'

"With startling understanding, I suddenly realized that I was doing a lot more than I had ever thought I was. I often felt inadequate about my *bikur cholim* activities, because I couldn't cook up delicious concoctions for the patients the way so many others could, nor could I do anything tangible to help care for patients like Edith, in an attempt to ease their dire situations. So I usually shrugged off my visits as insignificant. Yet Edith told me a completely different story on that memorable day. *Your visits make a difference to me*, was her message, and I walked out with my head held high and a simmering bubble of contentment within me.

"That was the last time I saw Edith. The next day was Shabbos, and when I went to visit her after Shabbos, I found out that she had passed away that afternoon." Deena concludes her account and lapses into silence.

"May I continue to be the visitor and not the visitee," she adds fervently.

PUTTING HER BEST FOOT FORWARD WITH *BIKUR CHOLIM*

Mimi Gross is another of my dedicated ladies. In addition to being on call for our group, Mimi visits a local hospital on a monthly basis, armed with a list of Jewish patients, which she receives from the chaplain's office.

"Twenty-five years ago," she explains, "a chaplain from Jewish Family and Career Services gave an intensive training session, and following that, participants in the session were allowed and encouraged to visit Jewish patients in the hospitals. I knew this was something I wanted to do. When my mother was sick with her final illness, I wasn't there for her in the ways I would have liked. Even when I was with her physically, which, in hindsight, wasn't often enough, I certainly wasn't there for her emotionally. I was busy with family responsibilities and grading students' papers... but the real truth was that I couldn't face the fact that my mother was preparing to leave this world, and so I kept myself emotionally at a distance from the entire situation. I decided to take the training session and then become a *bikur cholim* volunteer as a *zechus* for my mother's *neshamah*.

"It was my first visit. When I entered a patient's hospital room, my jaw dropped. I knew the person! And...she was catatonic (unresponsive to any stimulation), and simply stared vacantly ahead, just like my mother had done at the end. After wishing her a sincere *refuah sheleimah*, I walked out of the room and burst into tears.

"'How will you ever be able to do this mitzvah if you fall apart like this?' my friend Rivka, who had come with me, asked, putting an arm on my shoulder while I sobbed.

"But at the same time, I felt that this was my sign, a clear indication from Hashem, that my *teshuvah* had been accepted."

Five years of volunteering, of gowning up, donning rubber gloves, and radiating cheer, and Mimi felt she needed a break. Her family needed more of her time and energy, she decided, and so she began putting her hospital visits on the back burner.

Inexplicably, she developed severe pain in her foot, and no medicinal remedies seemed to be able to alleviate her distress. At a loss, she finally consulted an esteemed *rosh yeshivah* with whom she had a long-standing relationship.

"Where are you going?" he asked.

"To jazzercise," she confessed, unsure if the *rosh yeshivah* would approve of that form of exercise.

"No, no," he clarified. "Where are you *not* going? Did you stop going somewhere or doing something recently that might have some connection to why your foot began hurting?"

"Well," Mimi replied hesitantly, "I stopped my *bikur cholim* visits in the hospital recently…"

"Go back to doing them," the *rosh yeshivah* directed.

The day she resumed her *bikur cholim* visits, her foot pain stopped.

"*Bikur cholim* is an awesome responsibility," Mimi notes. She remembers going to see a patient who wanted her glasses. Having left them in a different area while undergoing a test, she couldn't see and felt terribly uncomfortable about it.

"I'll get them," Mimi offered, and trekked across the entire breadth of the hospital to find and retrieve the glasses. But that was just part and parcel of the mitzvah then…

"There are so many stories," Mimi tells me with a smile, remembering some of the poignant ones. "About a dozen years ago, I had this strong feeling that I should go to the hospital for a visit, even though it wasn't my regular day to go. When I arrived and glanced at my list, I found the names of two of my elderly neighbors, a husband and wife, there. I was able to visit them, and then the husband passed away a few days later. Boy, was I glad I had decided to go to the hospital on that day!

"Eleven years ago," Mimi continues, "I was given the ultimate test in *bikur cholim* when my husband, Tzvi *alav hashalom*, was diagnosed with malignant cancer. After his first surgery, the doctor told me that he wouldn't live for more than six months; they weren't able to remove all of the infected glands. I decided not to tell him. I wanted Tzvi to rebound, not to give up; I wasn't ready to lose him yet. For eight long months, I kept my first secret from my husband of almost forty years.

"The night before my husband's first chemotherapy session, a friend came over toting a large bag filled with treats, magazines, and puzzles. I hugged her, touched by her kindness. Transferring the goodies to a red-checkered picnic basket, I told Tzvi we were going on a picnic outing, and our positive attitude made such a difference.

"People did so much for us during the four years of Tzvi's illness. The visits, food, and phone calls meant the world to us. During his first hospitalization after surgery, our rabbi and *rebbetzin* popped in. 'We just wanted to make sure you were okay,' they said.

"Then the rabbi looked around and noticed the chair in the room. It was a lounge type of chair, and it had a flimsy cushion. 'You're going to sleep on that?' he asked, raising his eyebrows.

"I shrugged. 'It's fine.' Who could think about sleeping? My focus was on Tzvi.

"Within half an hour, a nurse came into the room, lugging a large cot with a comfortable mattress for me. I had no doubt that my rabbi and his wife had arranged this, and when Tzvi's hospitalization lasted for ten days, I was ever so grateful for their thoughtfulness.

"Years have passed. Tzvi outlived the doctor's prediction by three and a half years, and I know that each *tefillah* and mitzvah done in his *zechus* factored into his added time. The four years of Tzvi's illness ended up being the best, most meaningful four years of our very beautiful and cherished marriage. And now, each time

I step into the hospital corridor to visit another sick patient, I ask Hashem to consider it as a *zechus* for the memory of my dear parents and husband."

SHIDDUCH SERVICES

DID I EVER tell you I'm a *shadchante*? Considering that I've never made a single successful *shidduch*, although I have tried, allow me to explain: Bikur Cholim recently put out a newsletter, and in it, we mentioned our need for more volunteers. Mr. Krautman, an elderly widower, called to tell me how much he loved the newsletter. Then he asked how he could help.

Hmm, I mused. *Here's an individual who is bright and witty, but homebound...* Then epiphany struck.

There's another elderly gentleman, Mr. Peltz, who just called our shul recently. He had always been active and involved, but recently he's been struggling with various health issues, and unfortunately it has put him out of commission. He remarked to the secretary, "There should really be a system where shul members reach out to those of us who can't come anymore. I get really lonely..."

Strike for Bikur Cholim, I rued upon hearing about that conversation. *That's supposed to be our department...*

But now, I wondered if perhaps we could mend this tear.

"Mr. Krautman," I began, with mounting excitement. "How would you like to call Shmuel Peltz and check in on him every once in a while? He can't get out much, and I know that he's lonely and wants companionship. I bet a weekly call from you would really make him feel better."

"I'd love to do that!" Mr. Krautman exclaimed. "We're friends from way back, so I'll just tell him I was thinking about him, and we'll take it from there."

Perfect! I hung up and grinned.

So, you see, I'm not your stereotypical *shadchante*, at least not in the marriage department. But when you see the title on my résumé, you'll understand why it's there...

⌁⌁♡

THE BEST MEDICINE IN THE WORLD

A RETIRED CARDIOLOGIST and *chazzan*, Dan Appelrouth is a treasure. As a doctor, he was the rare breed who cared about every part of his patients' physical and emotional well-being. He once had a patient who was dying, and she had confided to him that she and her son, Sam, were embroiled in a relationship of conflict. It caused her great heartache.

While the woman was on her deathbed, Dan approached her, seeking to alleviate her pain.

"Mom?" he called softly. "It's me, Sam."

"Sam?" the patient echoed, her lips curving upward.

"Mom," Dan continued, "I know we've had our issues. I just want you to know that I forgive you, and I love you."

"I love you, too," she said. And she died with a smile on her lips.

Although officially Dan no longer works as a physician, he continues with his single-minded goal of mending broken hearts, giving the sick and needy the gifts of his time, love, and songs. When I worked as an activity director in an assisted living home, Dan would happily come and sing for our residents, lifting them out of their broken bodies, into a higher realm. The joy he brought was palpable and lasted even after his programs ended.

SARAH NEIDER WAS an elderly woman who loved the way Dan sang. She also had a love for the Yiddish language, and would sing Yiddish songs and speak Yiddish to her husband and to herself.

When Sarah was in the end stages of terminal cancer, she was in hospice, in a stupor. She hadn't communicated in three days, and everyone knew her end was near. Her devoted daughter-in-law, Kay, sought a means to bring comfort to her, and she put on a Dan Appelrouth CD that had some Yiddish songs on it. For the first time in three interminable days, Sarah opened her eyes and mouthed the words to the Yiddish songs. When the Yiddish songs ended, she closed her eyes and died.

HINDA GREENE WAS dying of cancer, and her husband, Chaim, was distraught. He would sit alone at Hinda's bedside day after day. Honing in on the need, Dan and his wife, Arlene, began to visit the couple, and tried to provide emotional support for the two of them, especially when Hinda went into a stupor.

Like Sarah Neider, Hinda, too, had always been a fan of Dan's singing. Now Dan sang his heart out to try and elicit some kind of response from Hinda. Tears rolled down Chaim's cheeks as he stared at his listless, unresponsive wife. Undaunted, Dan continued singing Hinda's favorite songs, but to no avail.

Arlene decided to help out. With her fingers, Arlene went up and down Hinda's forearm, stroking the older woman and speaking ever so gently to her. Suddenly, Hinda started making sounds, as if to communicate. Then she began to cry.

Arlene's touch, coming on the heels of Dan's singing, was the last thing Hinda responded to. She returned her soul to her Creator a few days later.

$\sim\!\!\!\sqrt{\!\!\sqrt{\!\!\!\sqrt{\!\!\!\sqrt{}}}}\heartsuit$

IN HIS RICH and melodious voice, Dan conveys his awe at the powerful human need for love and connection. "Sometimes," the good doctor says, "our love for others is the best medicine in the world for them."

$\sim\!\!\!\sqrt{\!\!\sqrt{\!\!\!\sqrt{\!\!\!\sqrt{}}}}\heartsuit$

SEEING THE WORLD THROUGH ROSE-COLORED GLASSES

TZIPPY BLACKMAN, ANOTHER devoted volunteer, could write her own book on *bikur cholim*. But she is so busy doing the mitzvah that I don't know when she would have the time.

"When I first started making hospital visits," Tzippy remembers, "I was scared to go into people's rooms. What if they didn't want me or it wasn't a good time? Now I'm much more comfortable doing my visits, and my experiences have been so enriching. So many patients I met came away stronger from their bouts with illness. It was like the illness gave them time to be with themselves, to contemplate their lives, to make improvements where necessary."

Tzippy recalls the time she knocked on someone's door and was invited in by the patient with a jovial, "Welcome to my condo!"

As Tzippy stared, the man began to explain, with a sparkle in his eyes. "You see, this is my hygiene area." He pointed to the sink. "And," he said, pointing to the tray near his bed, "this is my dining room.

"This is my bedroom," he continued, gesturing to his bed. Last, he indicated his wife, who was standing near the window, putting flowers in a vase, and concluded, "And this here is my rose garden."

Amazed, Tzippy replied, "I came to uplift you, but instead *you* uplifted *me* with your perspective."

The next year, when Tzippy was doing visits in the hospital, she found this same man's name on her patient list again. She went into his room with a smile, reminding him of that first time they'd met and how inspired she'd been by his positivity and good humor.

The man's eyes twinkled, and he pointed to a box of crackers sitting on the shelf near his window. "You can add this to the features in my condo," he said. "This is my pantry."

⁓⁓⁓♡

ANOTHER TIME, WHEN Tzippy went into a patient's room, she found the television blaring and the patient lying on her bed, listless. But after Tzippy introduced herself, the patient immediately perked up and became very bubbly and animated. She was a Holocaust survivor, and as Tzippy conversed pleasantly with her, she was awed that the woman could be so delightful even after enduring such suffering in her life. Although the woman was scarred from her experiences, tearing up when she mentioned her memories of her mother *bentching licht* and her father making Kiddush, she seemed to embrace life with such joy. It moved Tzippy and left her feeling very inspired.

⁓⁓⁓♡

THERE AT THE RIGHT MOMENT

AN INVALUABLE ASSET to our team and to Klal Yisrael, Mordechai Muller devoted many years to hospital visitation. Like a flaming candle, Mordechai ignited embers of light where there was darkness and despair.

He once walked into a room where a patient was on oxygen. The patient seemed to be in distress and was having difficulty breathing. Mordechai ran and found a nurse, who quickly came in and adjusted the patient's breathing apparatus. The man rested easily again. Mordechai had "just happened" to enter the room at the right moment.

AN ISRAELI PATIENT lay in the ICU, having suffered a concussion. He was breathing, but had not awakened in many days. His sister had flown in from Yerushalayim the night before to be with him. Distraught, she tried talking to her brother, attempting to wake him, but he remained unresponsive.

Mordechai found this Jewish patient on his hospital patient list and came in to see him. Knowing that the man didn't speak English, yet not knowing any Hebrew himself, Mordechai came up with the idea of *davening* aloud; after all, the *tefillos* in the siddur are in *Lashon Hakodesh*.

First Mordechai read *Ashrei* aloud. From there he proceeded to read other *perakim* of Tehillim. There was no movement from the patient. Asking the patient's sister for his name and their mother's name, Mordechai continued *davening* fervently and out loud for the man's recovery.

Just as he finished, the unbelievable happened: the patient opened his eyes. His sister spoke to him—and he responded to her! As the sister flew emotionally to her brother's side, Mordechai quietly left the room.

〜♡

MRS. COHEN WAS an eighty-nine-year-old woman, a Holocaust survivor whom Mordechai had known for decades. She had been brought to the hospital after a fall on her head.

For days, the doctors ran tests on her, trying to assess if Mrs. Cohen had sustained any brain damage. What made things difficult was the fact that Mrs. Cohen would partially awaken and open her eyes when people walked in, but she wouldn't say anything to acknowledge their presence. Without her speaking, the doctors had no way of ascertaining whether or not there was brain damage.

Then Mordechai walked in. When he heard the doctors' dilemma, he immediately approached the foot of the bed. Mrs. Cohen opened her eyes.

"Hello there, Mrs. Cohen," Mordechai said.

Without hesitation, Mrs. Cohen responded, "Oh, hello, Mordechai. I fell down some stairs and hit my head." From there she continued having a normal, coherent dialogue with Mordechai Muller, mentioning the Holocaust Museum where she was a regular speaker and how she hoped to be back speaking there again soon.

〜♡

WHEN SOME PATIENTS saw this seventy-ish-year-old man, white hair covered with a yarmulke, stick his head in the doorway and ask to come in, they'd respond, "We don't need a rabbi."

When Mordechai would tell them that he was not a rabbi, they might say something like, "Okay, but don't stay long." But then Mordechai would pull out a get-well card prepared by a child (the day school children would create these cards for volunteers to give to patients in the hospital) and say, "Here, this is for you," and almost always, the patient would melt.

One such patient was very sick, and he knew he didn't have long to live. Mordechai visited him several times over a period of two months. Each time, the patient looked forward to receiving a get-well card from Mordechai.

The day came when Mordechai met the patient's wife in the hallway, and she told him that her husband had passed away. In a voice choked with emotion, she said to Mordechai, "One of the last things my husband said was to tell you how much he appreciated getting those get-well cards from you."

ONCE, A PATIENT who was a WWII veteran confided to Mordechai, "I need to have my leg amputated from the knee down. I have a four-year-old grandson. He's always seen me walking normally on two good legs. He doesn't know about diseases, or why I won't be able to walk with him anymore, or why I will be missing part of my leg. I don't want to scare him away. I won't know what to tell him. What should I do?"

The words simply slipped out of Mordechai's mouth: "Tell him the truth."

The man was silent for a moment. Then he looked up at Mordechai and replied, "Of course. You're right. Thank you for reminding me of that."

BIKUR CHOLIM OF A DIFFERENT NATURE

AT FIRST I thought it was a loss that Ahuva would no longer be able to visit patients in hospitals and nursing homes, touching their lives with her unique brand of caring and light-hearted humor. Ahuva was one of our earliest and most dedicated volunteers, jumping on board with us from the time we first launched our organization. She was the rare individual who would complain when too much time went by without her hearing from us.

But then I realized that Ahuva *would* still be doing *bikur cholim*—it would just be of a much quieter and more selfless nature. She wouldn't be in the limelight anymore, nor would she get the same satisfaction or appreciation for her *bikur cholim* efforts. But the walls of her home would testify to her actions instead…

Let me backtrack. I had just received an email from Ahuva, informing Bikur Cholim that she would have to stop her volunteer activities for now. *My husband has Alzheimer's,* she wrote. *He needs me…*

I immediately raced to the phone. "Ahuva?" I began. "I am really sorry about your husband. This must be so hard for you."

"Yeah, well, I won't be able to do my volunteer work anymore. This is my new full-time job. Abie is a different person now, and it's a big adjustment. Sometimes he walks out of the house, and I have to run after him because he can get lost. Other times he wanders from room to room looking confused, as if he's lost something. I suppose he has. Can you imagine a spouse refusing to take a shower? Or get dressed? That's what I'm dealing with."

A laden silence stretched between us as I tried to absorb her intense pain. *How does it happen,* Ribono Shel Olam, *that a wonderful person, youthful, energetic, sparkling with life and intelligence, loses his vitality and withers, becoming a shell? How? And… why?*

"Listen, Ahuva, we're here if you need us. Please call if there's anything we can do. Take care—and Hashem should give you lots of strength."

A week later I called again to check in with her.

"Abie's doing much better," she told me, and I felt encouraged.

"In the Alzheimer's support group that I began to attend, they told me that sometimes rapid regression is caused by dehydration and malnutrition. The disease causes people to forget to eat, and they lose their appetite. So I spoke to the doctor. He put Abie on a new medication, and now he's a little more lucid. Sometimes we can even have a conversation, and I can almost forget… As far as his short-term memory, though, that's gone. But I figured out a way to use that to my advantage."

"Really?" I had to chuckle.

"I can ask him to do something one minute, and he'll refuse. But a minute later, I can try again and hope for a different response!"

"Good for you!" I laughed, glad that Ahuva was keeping her sense of humor.

"Also, Abie enjoys making Lego towers. So I have a whole bucket of Lego for him, to keep him engaged, you know. He gets a lot of pleasure from doing this. Then, when he leaves the room, I quickly dismantle the tower, and he doesn't recall doing it a moment ago. So he comes back to it refreshed, and enjoys the challenge of building all over again."

When our call was finished, I pondered the tragedy of a person losing his mind, *Rachmana litzlan*. The person's very essence dissipates, leaving in its wake a shell with vacant eyes.

Ahuva, hats off to you. Apparently your community bikur cholim *work was your training, building your muscles for the real "marathon" you now have to run. And I dare say that this private race of yours, where your every sinew and muscle is pushed to its limit, will lead directly to the portals of Gan Eden...*

PART 5

"CHAPLAINCY, THIS IS RACHEL. MAY I HELP YOU?"

*A*S THE YEARS passed and our children grew, it became clear to me and my husband that it was time for me to seek employment. Two rabbis in our community encouraged me to pursue hospital chaplaincy. They had both taken clinical pastoral education themselves, and they thought I would be well suited for the profession. They prodded me, "You're doing the job anyway; you may as well get it on paper and make it official."

Hmm—sounds interesting, I mused. To turn *bikur cholim* into a paid career?

With great trepidation, I began my two-year course in chaplaincy training. This included a total of three hundred clinical hours and one hundred educational hours (comprised of four hours of class time a week, plus regular meetings with our supervisors). During clinical hours, we had to visit patients on our assigned unit and then write progress notes about our visits. There was no official supervision during that time, but at our weekly classes or supervisory meetings, we discussed the visits, especially if there was anything that made us uneasy about any of them, and our supervisors provided guidance and advice.

It was a rigorous program, all things considered. But what I discovered one of my greatest challenges to be was explaining to other people exactly what kind of work I was doing. To my dismay, it seems that most people think of a "chaplain" as a kind of rabbi, when in reality, a chaplain's main goal is simply to provide emotional and spiritual support for someone going through trauma. He or she is encouraged to listen to others' stories or pain, show empathy, *daven* for them, and through this venue of sharing and caring, uplift them—that's all it is.

I received many confused, and sometimes hurtful, reactions when people heard what I was training for.

"You're training to be a—rabbi?" an esteemed *rebbetzin*, with whom I was close, inquired when I told her what I was doing.

"No, NO, NOOO!" That was the first and only time in the twenty-five years of my relationship with this *rebbetzin* that I raised my voice to her. I couldn't help it; the idea that this *chashuve* woman could entertain the thought, even for a moment, that I was *chas v'shalom* becoming a "rabbi" was simply too much to bear! "It's just paid *bikur cholim*, that's all," I explained firmly, my heart hammering in my chest as I silently begged her to understand. "I'm not, I would *never*, become a 'rabbi.'"

A friend teasingly asked me, "Should I call you Rabbi Stein?"

Why don't people understand? I wondered, glaring at her. *She's not serious, is she?* "Let's save that title for my husband, please, okay?" I replied.

$$\sim\!\!\!\!\!\sim\!\!\!\!\!\sim\!\!\!\!\!\heartsuit$$

WHEN YOU BEGIN to read these pages and hear about my chaplaincy training journey, you may be faced by many questions. How could I, a *frum* woman, sit with religious *goyim*, week after week, and not feel conflicted? How could I, an Orthodox Jew, watch nurses pull patients off of life support, and then be called to comfort the grieving families who had just killed their loved ones?

Understand that I had these questions and conflicts, too, as I traveled this tumultuous journey. I certainly felt like a sheep among wolves. But I really feel that these experiences built me into a stronger Jew. After four hours of sitting with ardent Christians every Monday morning for two years, I say *Aleinu* with more fervor than ever before. *Ashreinu mah tov chelkeinu*—How fortunate are we, and how good is our lot! We are so tremendously blessed to have the *Emes* with us.

Before embarking on this program, I consulted with my family's *rav*, and I was to be in touch with this *rav* on a constant basis throughout my training, as various questions and issues arose.

I remember the first troubling question I posed to the *rav*:

"What if they ask me to *daven*?" I asked. "Like, when I'm at a sick *goy's* bedside—what do I do?"

"So, *daven*," he answered. "There's nothing wrong with *davening* with a *goy* for his or her needs."

The only thing I was not allowed to do, the *rav* told me, was something that was contrary to halachah, such as a gentile ritual like baptizing a patient (not that I had any idea—or any desire to have any idea—about what *that* entailed!). I made this very clear to my supervisor from the start, and *baruch Hashem* she was okay with it.

And so, as I continued my involvement with our community Bikur Cholim, I simply added the chaplaincy training program to the rest of my schedule…

ON DIFFERENT WAVELENGTHS

"WHAT DO YOU mean, you won't do a baptism? All of the other chaplains do!" The young, pretty blonde nurse glared at me through narrowed blue eyes. *Shame on you for refusing to help this dying baby and his family in this way!* her expression screamed.

"I'm sorry, but my supervisor is aware that I can't do baptisms. I can pray with the family, support them, comfort them, but I am simply not allowed to do baptisms." My heart raced, but I made sure to keep my voice calm.

"Is it only Christians that you don't want to help, then?" A black nurse joined her blonde counterpart, her dark eyes spewing arrows of pure hatred.

"No, I am happy to help anyone. As I said, I can pray with people, comfort them, and support them, but baptism is a rite that I am not allowed to do."

"We understand," an older nurse stepped in and said, trying to mediate. "There are many different paths that lead to the same place."

"Well, I don't," the black nurse hissed, giving me that hateful stare again. I was glad to be surrounded by people; I would not have trusted her had we been alone. She looked like a volcano about to erupt.

"Would *you* do something that goes against *your* religion?" I asked her, trying to get her to understand my position.

"Well, no," she admitted, "but…"

PULLING THE PLUG

IN A HEART-STOPPING (unfortunately, quite literally) encounter during my first unit, I was called to attend to a family that had chosen to pull the plug on their ailing father.

So…I'm there to comfort the killers for murdering their father? I wondered, confused by the contradictions as I drove toward the hospital. This was the first time I was ever called in for an emergency, i.e., a patient who was dying, and I was, frankly, terrified of what awaited me in that hospital.

(In most of the units in which I was placed, I had to be in the hospital the whole time while I was on call. In this particular unit, though, chaplains on call were allowed to go home at night, as long as they took their pagers with them. As soon as the pager buzzed, indicating an emergency, the chaplain had to race over to the hospital—but that was fine with me, if it meant being able to sleep in my own bed that night, even if just for a few hours…)

The night was clear, crisp, and cold, one of those nights that invigorate you and make you feel glad to be alive. A myriad of stars twinkled down, the moon was a shining sliver, and I could feel Hashem's closeness to me. *Oh, Hashem, I'm so nervous; I need Your guidance so badly*, I thought as I sped along. For a change, I wished that some heavy traffic would suddenly appear and impede my progress to the hospital, but the roads were clear, and I arrived in record time.

"The man who's dying is in the Medical Intensive Care Unit," the nurse explained to me calmly. "It's his family who wants a chaplain. They pulled the plug on his respirator a little while ago, so it could happen any time."

You mean, "the man who's being killed by his family," I wanted to correct her, horrified by the whole situation. And the next comment that bubbled up inside me was: *What does this have to do with me?!*

I wanted to scream at this ignorant nurse, a nurse who thought she was calling a qualified chaplain. *Just because I'm on call and I'm supposed to be able to minister to dying patients and their families, doesn't mean I know the first thing about life and death! Especially when it's a murder case. I'm just a baby deep down, even though I'm already a grandmother a few times over, and I'm totally incapable of handling this kind of thing. I want my mommy...*

Now, get a hold of yourself, Chaplain, I commanded myself, making an effort to still the drumming of my heart. *You can do this, with Hashem's help, and you* will *do this. Hashem will guide you.*

Oh, please, Hashem, please let the right words come from my lips. Let this experience go well, I *davened* against the background echo of the clicking of my shoes as I walked through the deserted hospital hallways. Taking a deep breath, I forced myself to hurry toward the MICU. *I can't do this. Yes, you can, and you will.*

All too soon I arrived at the patient's room.

"Hi, I'm Chaplain Rachel," I said to the nurse there. "How are they doing?"

"Waiting," she replied.

I nodded, trying to feign calm as I clumsily donned the required yellow gown and rubber gloves before entering the sterile environment. I wondered cynically why it was necessary. After all, the man was going to die any minute. Did it really matter if he caught a germ or two? I felt like a large version of Donald

Duck as I braced myself, took a deep breath, and then knocked and entered the patient's room.

Sitting on two chairs facing the patient (whose name I saw was Owen) were his ex-wife, Barbara, who appeared to be in her early seventies, and his twenty-something-year-old son, Michael. Michael wore his long blond hair in a wild and unkempt manner, and he was dressed in a t-shirt and shorts despite the cold weather outside. Barbara's face appeared red and swollen, and she continued dabbing her eyes as she cried continuously throughout the evening. Owen appeared to be resting comfortably.

"Hello, I'm Chaplain Rachel, and I'm so sorry for what you're going through," I began the conversation.

"Hello, Chaplain, we're glad you could come," Michael responded. "I've already anointed my father and prayed over him, so he's got everything he needs."

Then Michael began a soliloquy that seemed to have no end, quoting passages from Matthew, Luke, and who knew what else. I felt like a fish that had suddenly swam up the wrong canal. Should I just admit ignorance? I wondered how he would react were I to say, "Hey, listen, I'm a Jewish girl; these are not my customs, nor am I familiar at all with them or with your bible." Or, since I was the only chaplain on call, was I supposed to play along, because really, my role was to be the comforter, no matter what the religion of the patient? That's what our supervisor always stressed in class. So I chose the latter path and kept nodding at Michael while he spouted his sewage, while inwardly I quaked. It was beyond awful.

Hashem, please tell me what You want from me now! I cried silently. I felt guilty, almost traitorous; was I right to pretend? Was I even being fair to these people who assumed I understood what they were talking about, who perhaps assumed I was someone I was not?

"Would it be okay if I go over and speak with your father for a moment?" I asked when Michael finally paused for a breath. "I'd like to let him know that we're all here."

I approached Owen, noting that his breathing was more labored now.

"Owen, I'm Chaplain Rachel. I want you to know that I'm here together with your loved ones, your son and Barbara. Owen, you're very sick right now. There's always the possibility that you'll recover, but there is also a chance that you won't. I want to wish you G-d's blessings at this time, and that everything should go smoothly for you."

I returned to my seat near Michael and Barbara.

"Barbara, you seem so distraught." I felt she needed a chance to open up.

"I just feel so guilty," she told me. "You know, even though we divorced, we still very much cared for each other. Neither of us ever remarried. Owen used to call me all the time, sometimes many times a day. And I would help him, shop for him, shuttle him to appointments…

"Well," she paused, "the day he had this stroke, he must've called about twenty times! That last time he called, I didn't answer, because I was worn out. But had I answered that call, maybe I could have saved his life. He needed me…"

"So you're feeling weighed down; you feel like you could have done more. Like you should have answered that phone call," I said.

Barbara nodded, as hot tears streamed down her face.

"I wonder, Barbara, if you can give yourself a gift. It sounds to me like you went beyond the call of duty and helped Owen a lot. Can you possibly tell yourself, 'I did the best I could with the tools I had'? Of course, had you been a mind reader, you would've picked up that twenty-first call. But you're human. And you gave your all. That's more than most of us can say." Barbara nodded, her eyes fixed on mine.

"Maybe," she said.

Owen began coughing intensely now, and the coughs racked his body, but the two family members seemed oblivious. I, however, was petrified. Was this the death rattle I had learned about?

"Can I call a nurse?" I asked, my stomach performing flip-flops. When Michael and Barbara agreed, I ran to get a nurse, and she gave Owen some meds and suctioned him to ease his discomfort.

"What really worries me is whether or not my father will go to Heaven," Michael said when the nurse left. "You see, he did some awful things in his life. And I don't know if he repented."

I felt uncomfortable with this turn of the conversation. A person's hearing is the last sense to go, and it seemed in really poor taste to discuss Owen's sins while he was breathing his last breaths. But when I suggested that we leave the room to continue talking in this vein, they were not interested. They wanted to remain right where we were.

"So you're worried he might not get in?" I asked softly.

"My father was a drunken bum," Michael told me. "He was vile, abusive, and cursed all the time. And he never told me he loved me. That's why my mom finally left him; he was ruining our lives. But I told him I forgave him. And I told him I love him. Years later, he told me he loved me. Just not when I was growing up."

"That was good of you to tell him you forgave him and that you love him. And I'm happy for you that he finally told you that he loved you. Every child needs to hear that," I said. "Now, is there anything you can do for your father, since you're worried about his afterlife? You're his legacy, after all; if you do good deeds and pray, might that help him?"

Barbara smiled; she seemed to like my Jewish ideas.

"I told you already," Michael insisted. "I anointed him and prayed over him. And who knows? Maybe he did repent. Maybe he'll be okay."

After three hours of listening to New Testament quotes and ideas, my head was spinning and I was feeling nauseous. I wanted to go home. I was a Bais Yaakov graduate; my husband was a rabbi. I had never been exposed to—this. Michael really took over the bulk of the conversation; he seemed to enjoy hearing himself speak. And his mother just listened to him and rarely offered her own opinions.

Suddenly, Owen coughed so fiercely that it propelled him up into a sitting position. I ran to get the nurse. Once again, she administered treatment, and Owen relaxed.

"Would it be okay if I said a prayer?" I asked. Barbara and Michael nodded. I extracted my Hebrew-English Tehillim, hoping they wouldn't notice the Hebrew part.

I read *perek chaf-gimmel* in English.

"Is that Hebrew?" Michael asked.

"Yes," I answered, my heart hammering.

"You read Hebrew?"

"Yes," I admitted.

And then came the clincher: "Are you Jewish?"

"Yes, I am. Forgive me, please, for not telling you that earlier. I was not trying to be deceptive. But seeing what an ardent Christian you are, I was concerned that you wouldn't feel comforted if you knew I'm Jewish."

Michael's face turned beet red. He looked like he was going to explode. But after a few moments, he composed himself.

"Well, no wonder you didn't seem familiar with some of the things I mentioned. I was starting to wonder what kind of chaplain you were. So let me ask you a question. About Adam and Eve…"

We stood there, at Owen's bedside, discussing *Chumash* for about ten minutes. Finally I felt that I was on my own turf! Though I couldn't forget that I stood in the presence of a man who was breathing his last breaths in this world.

I finally ended the conversation by wishing both Michael and Barbara strength and comfort. Barbara clasped my hands and held them for a long time.

I slowly walked back down that silent corridor and out of the hospital, berating myself all the while. Why hadn't I told them right away that I'm Jewish? Had I done wrong? Had I disappointed Hashem by not readily admitting that I am a Jew?

When I discussed this incident later with my supervisor, she told me that I'd done nothing wrong by not telling Owen's family earlier that I'm Jewish. She said that when Michael asked me if I was Jewish, I should have just said yes, which I did, and then I should have asked him if there was anything he needed that I couldn't offer. "You should not have apologized," she said. "There was no need for that. Rachel, that's what chaplaincy is all about—respect for all faith traditions. I wouldn't go into a Jewish patient's room and apologize to him for being Christian. I would simply see how I could be of help, regardless of my personal religion. So why would you need to apologize for being Jewish?"

Thoughts of Moshe Rabbeinu swirled through my mind then. Why was he not *zocheh* to burial in Eretz Yisrael? One reason given (*Devarim Rabbah* 2:8) is because he didn't readily admit his *Yiddishkeit* when he was a fugitive from Mitzrayim; he dressed as an Egyptian, and the daughters of Yisro took him to be an Egyptian man. Yosef Hatzaddik, on the other hand, readily admitted to being a Jew during his exile, and therefore he was *zocheh* to be buried in Eretz Yisrael.

My guilt was overwhelming, thudding and pounding me mercilessly. I am a Jew, and I am proud of being a Jew. I had just felt pushed against a wall in a very unusual situation, and that was why I had blurted out my apology…

But that night, as I drove home from the hospital at nearly 1:00 a.m., I was able to set aside my guilt, at least momentarily, in order to marvel at the disparity between the nations of the world and Klal Yisrael. For a *frum* Jew, every moment of life is sacred. We would never consider touching a plug that could spell the difference between life and death. Those decisions are up to our Creator, not us.

As I entered my own warm home and put up the kettle to boil, I thought about what I could sustain from this unique experience. My feeling of gratefulness to be a Jew had been strengthened, that was for sure. To know exactly what is expected of us in each stage of our lives, to have an unambiguous roadmap from the *Ribono Shel Olam* to guide us through our every waking second, is such a gift. Our *Emes* is so pristine and clear, especially when held up to the tinsel of *sheker* that I had been exposed to that evening.

I gazed out the window at the sparkling stars and glowing moon as I said a *Shehakol*, slowly and purposefully, before sipping my steaming tea. "Thank You, Hashem," I whispered. "Thank You for taking care of me and for making me a part of Your beautiful, miraculous world. Thank You, Hashem, for making me a Jew."

STEPPING UP TO THE PLATE

I CONTINUED THE course, doing my clinical visits, but the chaplain title still didn't seem to fit comfortably. After all, I was just a mother and a *bikur cholim* volunteer. Chaplain Rachel? It sounded too strange, too formal. Our supervisor, however, insisted that we introduce ourselves as "Chaplain," novice students that we were notwithstanding.

But just a short while into the program, there came a day when I mustered all of my confidence and actually introduced myself with the title "Chaplain." A twenty-year-old *frum* boy in our community was incarcerated in jail and was being denied kosher food. All prisoners must dress the same and eat the same, was the jail's rule. No special privileges for anyone. His mother was appealing to anyone who could help, desperate for her child's welfare.

I am an innately shy person, and I also harbor a fear of policemen and the power they wield. Yet I had a feeling that I could help out in this situation. And so, with shaking hands, I picked up the phone and called the jail.

"This is Chaplain Rachel," I said in an authoritarian tone. *Good girl*, I goaded myself on. You *can do this!* "I'm calling about prisoner Z."

"Yes, Chaplain?" the jail warden asked respectfully.

"Mr. Z. must have kosher food. It is a religious obligation for Jewish people to eat kosher; they are not allowed to eat the standard fare that is given to everyone else. I am calling to ascertain that Mr. Z.'s needs will be met."

"Chaplain, our inmates' well-being is our primary concern. Mr. Z. will get his kosher food. Thank you for calling."

"Thank you, sir," I answered. "Will he get it today?"

"Yes, Chaplain, right away."

Way to go, Chaplain! Hanging up the phone, I danced a little jig in my kitchen and hummed my way into supper preparations.

-⌁⌁♡-

TO BE FIXING CARS AND WORKING IN MY GARDEN

Mr. G., a soldier, was two days away from being deployed to Afghanistan when he was suddenly diagnosed with leukemia. I had heard about him from another chaplain, and went to pay him a visit myself one day.

After knocking and entering the room, I found Mr. G. reading while sitting in a chair close to the window. His private room was well lit and clean. He exuded a strong energy, and looked the picture of vitality and health. The only giveaway about his condition was the fact that he was in the hospital and that there was an IV line connected to his arm.

"Good morning, Mr. G. Are you up for some company?" I greeted him.

He gave me a welcoming smile and quickly put down his newspaper. "Sure, any time."

"I'm Chaplain Rachel," I introduced myself.

"How ya doing today, Chaplain?"

"Fine, thank G-d. How are *you* is the more important question."

"I'm fine," he said, smiling thinly. "I was just re-admitted for a stronger round of chemotherapy than what they gave me the last time. They were supposed to start it yesterday, but I was running a fever, so they didn't. They wanted to send me home, but I told them, 'No, I'm not going back home and coming back again in another two weeks. Just keep me here and let's get this treatment moving.' So I'm hoping they're going to start it today."

"I hope so, too," I replied. "Are you worried about the way you'll react to a stronger dose?"

"Nah, I can take it. It'll be okay. I'm not scared. As long as the doctors are hopeful and know what they're doing, then I'm fine. It's if they start to wonder and worry and scratch their heads, then I'll worry.

"They're supposed to do a spinal tap and a bone biopsy today. Now there's some pain in those procedures; I know, 'cuz I had them before, and believe me, there's pain. I'll be awake the whole time. I'm not scared of the pain; I just want to get it over with. I wish they would come already, so I could get it over with."

I don't believe you're not scared of the pain; if that were really the case, you wouldn't be talking about it so much.

"Well, it must be that the doctors are hopeful if they're planning to give you a stronger dose of chemo. Sounds like they feel there's a good chance of knocking that cancer out of your system. But I understand what you're feeling; waiting around is hard."

"Yeah, but I'm not scared of the pain. Even though I'll be up during the procedures. Like I said, I just want to get this over with. I wish they would just come already."

"I hope they'll be here soon," I said again.

"I told my wife not to come to the hospital," Mr. G. continued. "It's so far, and she has to work. So I told her to just come on the weekend when she's off, unless there's an emergency. I'll be fine."

I nodded, thinking to myself, *Phooey! Did she have to listen to him?* I wished Mr. G. had not taken the martyr role and told his wife not to come. He really seemed to need some support. Clearly, he was terrified of his upcoming tests and the inevitable pain, but he wanted to show a strong face by denying his fear. Every one of the numerous times he said, "I'm not scared," I could almost see the bold print suspended above him, screaming out, "I'm scared out of my wits!" Not only that, but when a person thinks about how painful something is going to be, it automatically makes him feel the pain even more.

I wondered about the best way to encourage Mr. G. and address his fears.

"Mr. G., would you like to hear some suggestions of things I might try to concentrate on if I had to undergo a painful procedure?"

Mr. G.'s face lit up. "That'd be great."

"Well, I would hold onto the bed or maybe a nurse's hand, if that's available, and imagine that I was holding the hands of my loved ones. I would imagine the love and concern pouring out of their hearts into mine, and that would comfort me. After that, maybe I would picture a beautiful sunrise or sunset, or imagine myself on the beach near the ocean. And I would pray. I would pray that G-d guide the hands of the doctors to perform the test easily but effectively, and in the least painful way. I would pray that G-d give the doctors the wisdom to act as His emissaries and help these procedures become a tool to aid in my healing. How does that sound to you?"

"All that stuff sounds great. The loved ones, the nature, and especially the praying. Thank you, Chaplain. I'm going to keep those things in mind."

Mr. G. was silent for a moment, and then he said, "Chaplain, you know what else is really hard about this whole thing? It's not the pain and the procedures; I can handle all that. But I hate being cooped up."

"You feel almost like a prisoner." I nodded. I also hate being cooped up. "That's rough. What do you like to do in your normal life?"

"I love to be outside." Mr. G. glanced out the window, as if picturing himself doing his normal activities. "I work on fixing cars, and I love to work in the garden. I'm outside all the time."

"So that makes your hospital stay even harder."

"Sure does."

"Can you at least go out of this room, walk the halls or something?"

"Oh, sure. I go downstairs, get something from the cafeteria, anything to get out of this room."

"Well, I hope one day soon you'll be back to fixing those cars and working in that garden of yours," I said.

"Me, too." He looked at his watch, frowning. "I sure hope they come soon."

"Me, too. Mr. G., would you like me to pray with you?"

"I'd love that."

And so I began my prayer. "G-d, please guide the hands of the doctors today during the tests that Mr. G. will undergo. May they be with as little pain as possible, and please help the doctors use the knowledge from these tests to help Mr. G. have a full recovery to good health as soon as possible. Please give Mr. G. the strength he needs to get through the ordeals of his illness. And please help him get back on his feet, so that he can continue to live the life that he loves—fixing cars, working the land, and feeling productive."

"Thank you, Chaplain," Mr. G. said gratefully.

"My pleasure. Feel good, Mr. G., and all the best to you."

I felt saddened by Mr. G.'s situation: a forty-two-year-old man fighting a life-threatening illness while the world continued to move on outside as if everything were normal. Illness is always devastating, but it seems even more tragic when it hits a young person.

From Mr. G.'s reaction to my prayer, though, it seemed that it had helped soothe him a bit. Perhaps it made him realize that G-d is in control of his illness, and that He can effect a cure according to His will. And isn't that always the goal of *tefillah*—to teach us how every aspect of our lives is in the hands of Hashem?

MY MISSING SENIOR

DURING THIS TIME, at the beginning of my chaplaincy training program, I was also doing some work as an activity director in the local, Jewish assisted living home. My chaplaincy supervisor kindly allowed me to use the hours I spent working there to complete my clinical-hour requirement for my program.

Sylvia was one of my favorites at the assisted living home. Crowned with a head of soft white hair, she was kind, friendly, and smart, with a generous spirit. Her cerulean blue eyes twinkled with a love of life and people. To my sadness, toward the second year of my employment in the assisted living home, Sylvia began to decline, as she became caught in the claws of dementia.

It was Wednesday, senior citizens' discount day, and it was my job as activity director to take our residents shopping. Every week we would lumber into our fifteen-seater bus, hoisting canes and walkers. Only the more able-bodied residents would come, and it was a pleasant change for all of them to get out and have some varied scenery. The residents relished the independence of choosing their own groceries, and a cheerful mood permeated the air as I revved up the motor and pulled out of the parking lot.

Our normal protocol was for everyone to meet me at the front of the store after about half an hour of shopping. So far, every Wednesday's trip had been smooth and uneventful. Until that day…

At first, all seemed to go as planned. The residents shopped, and at the designated time, I found them waiting for me at the front of the store, clutching carts loaded with groceries. I told them I'd be right there, and went to pull up the bus to the store entrance. Jumping out, I offered a helping hand to whoever needed it. Grocery bags were duly loaded, seatbelts were buckled, and I took inventory.

"Has anyone seen Sylvia?" I asked.

"I thought she was in the check-out just behind me," Norman said.

A few minutes passed, and there was still no sight of Sylvia.

"Where is she already?" Joe grumbled. "We're gonna be late for lunch."

"If you don't mind waiting here, I'll just run in and find her," I said to the group. "I'll be right back."

Can one offer tzedakah *to Rabi Meir Ba'al Hanes to find a missing senior?* I wondered.

"Did you happen to see a white-haired lady wearing a blue sweater?" I tremulously asked a store employee, my voice sounding panicked even to my own ears.

"Yeah," the woman said thoughtfully, wrinkling her eyebrows. "She went thatta way."

I offered a quick thanks and charged off in the direction her finger had indicated.

But Sylvia was not there. I looked up and down each aisle in the store. No Sylvia. My heart began pounding staccato beats, and I pictured the front page headlines: "Activity Director Loses Senior Resident on Grocery Trip."

"But, officer," I would protest, picturing a stern-faced officer

slapping cold handcuffs onto my wrists, "she was here a moment ago. It's not my fault..."

"Have you seen a white-haired lady, blue sweater, glasses?" I pleaded with another employee as I flagged him down. *Please say yes*, I *davened*.

Oh, Sylvia, what I would do to hear one of your family stories right now, along with your gentle laughter and twinkling blue eyes. You always have a kind word to say and a cheerful way in which to view any situation. And sometimes you just want a hug, and then you thank me afterward as if I've given you the greatest gift.

"I thought I saw her go out," the employee said, meeting my eyes. I saw my fear mirrored in his gaze and began to run toward the glass sliding doors. I chugged up and down through the sea of cars in the parking lot, hoping to see Sylvia's slight, stooped form. All the while, thoughts chased each other in my mind: *Will I have to call the police? Is Sylvia okay? And is it okay to leave the other residents sitting inside the bus unattended while I search for her? But—what other choice do I have?*

"Excuse me," I said to a whistling store employee who was gathering abandoned shopping carts. "My seniors are inside that bus over there while I'm trying to find one more of our residents. Would you mind just keeping an eye on them, please? You know, in case they need something?"

"No problem." He tipped his hat and headed toward the bus.

"Looking for someone?" a passerby who was loading his groceries into his trunk asked as I ran by.

"An old lady, white hair, blue sweater—"

"Glasses and a walker?" he finished, and I almost cried with relief.

"She was sitting inside the store when I saw her," he continued, "in the floral department."

"You saved my life," I told him.

And there, amid the red roses and gardenias, sitting calmly at a round table, was Sylvia.

"Oh, is it time to go?" she asked innocently, greeting me with her typical smile.

"Sure is," I answered, helping her up.

"Aren't these flowers beautiful?" she murmured. "This is my favorite place in the whole store. I was tired, so I just sat down to take a little rest."

I hope you got some for both of us, my dear. I walked calmly alongside my charge, willing my heart to slow to a normal pace.

I settled Sylvia into her seat, thanked the kind store employee for watching over my busload these past few minutes, and practically fell into the driver's seat.

"Fly me to the moon," Paul belted out cheerfully in his usual, off-tune key.

Only if you take me with you, I thought, maneuvering through the traffic. *I could use a vacation after this.*

"Okay, Paul, prepare for take-off. We're going."

"Really?" he said, his brown eyes twinkling. "Fly me to the moon…"

I sighed with relief when we pulled up to the entrance of the assisted living home. Passengers were unloaded, groceries were brought in, and the activity director teetered, on the verge of collapse.

"How was your trip?" Janet, my boss, greeted me with her usual warm smile.

"Well, I could tell you it was fine," I began, "and everything *is* fine now. But—well, let me think how to tell you this… Sylvia disappeared."

Janet gaped at me, her mouth forming an open circle of shock.

"No worries," I added quickly. "She's home, safe and sound. But I think I'd like a caregiver to come with me from now on. Just to have an extra set of hands."

"Great idea." Janet nodded. "Honestly, Rachel, one day our staff will write a book with all of our senior stories from the last twenty-plus years. It'll be a bestseller."

"I'll bet." I grinned. "I was going to ask you, since I just aged about twenty years in the past hour—do you have a spare room for me here, maybe next to Sylvia?"

Janet walked around her desk and enveloped me in a soothing, motherly hug. "All in a day's work," she said softly. "Go get yourself some coffee and relax. You'll be okay."

I planned to do just that, but not before checking the mirror as I walked down the hall to see how many extra wrinkles I'd brought home from our small outing to the store.

WAY TO GO, NORMAN!

AND THEN THERE was Norman. Norman, whose whole face became wreathed in smiles when something made him happy. Years ago, he had been an artist, and many of his scenic paintings adorned his walls. Norman still loved to paint, and he was very meticulous about painting inside the lines. Most of the time, though, he stared vacantly into space, not really aware of his surroundings.

"Norman, want to play Wii with some of us?" I invited him one afternoon.

Norman nodded and then shuffled along as we made our way into the activity center. I formed teams, and we proceeded to play bowling. There was only one snag. Norman refused to give up his remote so that others could take a turn. When I tried convincing him, he glared at me and stomped his foot. He wasn't sure what to do with the device while holding it, but he knew that he did not, under any circumstances, want to relinquish it.

Suddenly I had a brainstorm. "Here, Norman," I said, handing him a remote that was not connected to the system. Once I'd given him another remote, Norman was happy to hand over the first one.

"Your turn," I called to Edward, as ten new pins appeared on the screen.

When it was Norman's turn, I stepped behind him, holding the working remote.

"Go ahead, Norman," I urged pleasantly, as I prepared to bowl for him.

As Norman pushed the buttons on his inert remote, I got a strike.

"Good job, Norman! You got a strike! Way to go!"

Norman chuckled, proud of his accomplishment. And I laughed along.

Part of my heart felt proud of my creative maneuvering; I had successfully pulled the wool over Norman's eyes to keep him happy while helping everyone else continue playing. But the other chambers in my heart squeezed in sadness and a touch of remorse: if only Norman was fully in control of his mental capacity, this kind of innocent deception wouldn't be necessary...

HOLD THE POISON

THERE WAS ONE resident in the assisted living home who was paranoid that someone was trying to poison her.

"What would you like for lunch?" the dietician asked her as

he made his regular rounds one day.

"Chicken and rice," Lena said. "Are you going to poison me?"

"One chicken and rice for Lena," Shimon called to the kitchen staff. "But hold the poison."

MIRACLE IN OUR DAYS

ANNA HADN'T SPOKEN in years. Severely physically and mentally handicapped, when she turned her head or tried to move any body part, it seemed to rotate in slow motion. Although we included her in activities, we would always wrap our hands around hers to help her participate.

One day I arranged for a singer to entertain the residents. A retired doctor and *chazzan* in our community, Dr. Dan used his musical talents to do *chessed* and to raise money for *tzedakah*. As he regaled the group of seniors with song after song, the residents joyfully sang along, tapping their feet and clapping. And that was when I saw a miracle.

Anna's lips were moving, and as I moved toward her, I saw that she was mouthing the words of the songs. Who said we don't see miracles these days?

A MOTHER'S PAIN

SOMETIMES MY DAYS seemed to meld into my nights, with my Bikur Cholim responsibilities forming an extension to my chaplaincy training. Once, after spending the night on call in the hospital during my second unit, I went to visit Miriam.

Miriam's teenage daughter had been hospitalized because she

had suffered a nervous breakdown, and Miriam, a single mother, was beside herself.

"Rachel," she cried, as we stood outside her daughter's room, "I don't know what to do! They want her to have shock treatment, but I'm so scared. I'm scared that it will take her memory. I don't want it to take her memory away."

"The treatment is good," one patient from across the lunch table piped in. "I've had it three times. It really helps. And when I woke up, I knew who I was right away."

"Miriam, what do the doctors say?"

"They are advocating for this treatment," she said. "But what if it hurts her? I'm just so tired. Tired of everything, of handling every single situation singlehandedly. Why is every crisis mine alone to handle? Why did I ever get divorced? I thought it would make life easier to get out of a bad marriage, but life is so much more complicated without any support."

"I'm so sorry," I ventured.

Miriam peered into her daughter's room and gestured toward the girl sitting listlessly in bed, dressed in a yellow hospital gown and staring vacantly.

I swallowed hard, imbibing the volumes of pain in her heart. When she burst into gut-wrenching sobs, I held out my arms, and she folded into my embrace until the storm subsided.

I finally left Miriam, and resolved to try and visit again the following week. *What some people go through*, I mused, shaking my head as I walked down the corridor.

I was unprepared for the feeling of relief that coursed through me when the nurse buzzed me out of the psychiatric ward. I took a moment to simply breathe in the air of the free world, grateful for my health and for the reminder, once again, of how very much I have to be thankful for.

UNIT TWO, HERE I COME!

IN ORDER TO get full certification as a chaplain, which would enable me to work in hospitals, nursing homes, or hospices, I had to accrue four units of clinical pastoral education. So, after finishing my first unit in a veterans' hospital, off I went to begin my second unit—this time in a children's hospital.

To say I was overwhelmed the first week doesn't begin to touch on the situation. The program mandated eight hours of clinical visitation per week, a one-hour supervisory meeting, and four hours of class work. In addition to all that, we had to sleep at the hospital three times a month for sixteen-hour shifts, and one time a month for a twenty-four-hour shift.

My family is not going to like this, I thought. At the veterans' hospital, I was only on call twice a month. Plus, I never had to sleep over there; I got to take a pager home for whenever emergencies arose.

Our orientation took a full week, from 8:30 a.m. until 5:00 p.m. every day. One night I had to shadow a resident chaplain until 9:00 p.m.!

On that occasion, I remember shaking when I followed the resident chaplain into our first patient's room. Stevie was seventeen and lay in the hospital bed, pale and listless, attached to an I.V. Somehow, all I could think of as I stared at this teenager and blinked back tears, was, *I also have two beautiful sons around that age, one sixteen and one seventeen… Oh, please, Hashem, please keep them healthy…*

Unit two was a much more intense program than unit one. Would I survive it? I had my doubts. I actually considered quitting, but I kept telling myself to give it a few weeks. If the program did not become livable by that point, I would stop and say, "My family and life come first."

I cried a lot that first week of the program. On the night that was the hardest, that "forever day" when I had to stay until nine, I walked into the chaplaincy office and began to explore a little. I was stunned to find several Hebrew-English siddurim there. Opening one, I read the inscription inside:

Wishing you a speedy recovery and a complete return to good health! Our tefillos are with you at this time.

Michele Asa and Rachel Stein

Bikur Cholim of Atlanta

If this wasn't a meteor streaking straight from Heaven, showing me that Hashem was nodding His approval at me, even while I was on this difficult journey, I didn't know what was.

"Look!" I burst into the office of the chaplain on staff, beaming a 1000-watt smile. "Remember I told you about my little organization that a friend and I run together? Well, here we are!"

I held out the siddur for her to read the inscription.

"Very nice, Rachel." She gave me a smile before going back to her computer.

For me it was more than "very nice." It was the beginning of my decision to stay put and work my way through the unit.

THE DARKEST POINT OF NIGHT

My first experience with a dying child…

Heartbroken, I joined the mother, her sisters, the grandparents, great-aunts, and even the great-grandmother in their grief.

A baby. Ribono Shel Olam, *why is this baby dying?* I wondered, tears sliding down my cheeks. To my consternation, I found out that the baby was a victim of child abuse. I discovered later that the baby's twin sister, in the ICU, too, was also a victim of abuse. She, however, was slated for life. The father was arrested, while the mother would return home with empty arms. DFACS would take the surviving baby girl away from her, declaring her incapable and unfit to care for children. And it was my job now to comfort the family. What in the world could I say? "I'm sorry you decided to abuse your children"?

The pain washed over me in waves as my tears flowed together with those of the family. "You know," I began softly, "at the darkest point of night, daybreak is about to begin. May G-d give you strength."

Toward the end of the visit, I placed my hands on the dead baby's head and whispered a prayer to Hashem that this pure, little soul, who had finished his mission in life in so short a time, have peace.

Even when I returned home the next day to the warmth and familiarity of my own family, my tears continued. I saw that innocent baby wherever I turned. So precious, so pure, and such a short journey on this earth. Why? Only Hashem, in His infinite wisdom, knows why. Our job is to continue to walk and trust in Him.

A WORLD GONE MAD

A WORLD GONE mad... A three-year-old child was brought in with multiple stab wounds. Why would anyone hurt an innocent baby?!

While the doctors fought for the child's life, I *davened*, my heart pounding. When the family members arrived, I tried to offer a comforting presence to them as they waited, praying for life, while their world spun like a cyclone on a deadly path of destruction.

A police officer arrived to speak with the family. The mother's friend was suspected of committing the crime, and they were asked to describe the person's appearance. By the next day, the friend was apprehended, but the true story of what had happened was out: The child's father, who had been admitted for stab wounds to a different hospital, was indicted for killing two of his children, a fifteen-month-old and the three-year-old's twin brother, and for stabbing the third, the child brought to our hospital. Indeed, a world gone mad…

I LOVE YOU, KAREN

Karen was a fifteen-year-old girl with a feeding tube who was unable to swallow. We talked and played cards, and I spoke to her mother. I learned that Karen was going to be transferred to a psychiatric hospital, as the doctors felt that her condition was induced by an inability to handle stress.

"Can you believe this?" Karen fumed to me, spitting into a cup. "Just because I can't swallow, they treat me like I'm crazy?"

I felt a surge of anger as I pondered the injustice of this. Why *didn't* the doctors believe her? Why did they insist that she was in need of treatment for her mind, when it seemed so clear that all that ailed Karen was a physical issue? She presented herself as a normal, coherent, and intelligent young lady.

But I was to learn a good lesson in letting go of my naiveté and looking more deeply at a situation in front of me.

Karen had confided to me that her parents were divorced, and that her father had hardly anything to do with her. He never called; he never told her, "I love you."

Until the afternoon when I was there and her cell phone rang.

I saw a big smile appear on her face when she heard the voice on the other end. A moment later, I heard her say, "I love you, too, Dad," and when she looked up at me, her smile had grown even wider.

Hmm… I wondered. Perhaps the doctors were really on to something, after all? Perhaps there really *was* a psychological element involved in Karen's inability to swallow—namely, her desperate need for her father's attention?

Perhaps all the hullaballoo was worth it, after all, if it got Karen's father to give her what she so badly craved?

I held Karen's hand for a long time and wished her the very best. I prayed with her and encouraged her…and I resolved to say "I love you" more often to my own brood and let them know that I was always there for them.

〰♡

THE MAN WITH THE GOLDEN TEETH

"Chaplain, you're a woman of G-d," Dave, a black father, said to me, as he gently rocked his sick two-year-old back and forth. "Let me hear what you have to say about this."

I found myself entranced by his gold teeth that sparkled every time he spoke; he had at least three in the top front part of his mouth, or was it four?

"My wife might seem to be the sweetest person you've ever met. 'Pray for my baby,' she says. 'Pray for my husband.' And she looks at you with those big, innocent eyes. But inside she's wicked through and through, and I can't take it anymore! She curses at me, threatens me, kicks me out of the house. Do I have to take that? I want out of this marriage. What do you say to that?"

I sighed. *Hashem, I need Your help!* I silently implored.

"I'm sorry it's so hard for you," I started to say. "Have you tried counseling?"

"For me?" He looked appalled.

"Well, marital therapy is for couples. I usually advocate trying whatever you can do to save the marriage, for your sake and the sake of the children. Then, if that doesn't work…"

"I don't need counseling! It's all her, I tell you. Let me show you some of her text messages. You don't know me, so why should you believe me? And here, listen to some of her voicemails. What do you think of that?"

The language was unspeakable. I was horrified.

"Listen, Dave. You certainly don't have to allow yourself to be abused."

"All I want is to be a father to my children, but I need out of this marriage."

I nodded, realizing that he didn't really want advice. He just needed to vent, and he wanted me to sanction his decision to divorce his wife. I opted not to sanction any decision, but just tried to provide him with a listening ear.

After about thirty minutes of reflective listening, I said, "G-d bless you, Dave. I wish you lots of strength and wisdom, good health for you and your children, and happiness in the future. All the best to you." And I left the room, gently closing the door behind me.

So marriage counseling is also part of this deal, huh? My thoughts swirled as I eagerly headed toward the serenity of the chaplain's office. *You just never know what you'll find inside these rooms…*

LIKE SORE THUMBS

"Hey, Rachel," a black peer of mine, Debra, grabbed my attention when we were together for our weekly class session. "I really want to learn about all religions, know what I mean? Can you give me the name of your church so I can go?"

Doesn't sound so kosher to me, I thought, wondering what to say to her. Wouldn't it be a mockery of a shul to welcome a *goy* who just wanted to come there as a spectator?

"Let me get back to you," I stalled. "I'll ask my husband."

"Why should it be a problem?" my husband said, when I sat down to ask him about it. "The *pasuk* in *Yeshayah* says, *Ki beisi beis tefillah l'chol ha'amim*, that Hashem's House is a House of prayer for *all* the nations. So a *goy* can come into a shul. And actually, people do it all the time."

"They do?" I said, aghast. I guess I wouldn't know; I don't go to shul that often myself.

The following week, when I came into class, I gave Debra the address of our shul, as well as a list of do's and don'ts.

"Long sleeves, long skirt, and cover the collar bone. Go straight to the women's side of the divider. And...let me know how it goes, okay?"

Next week... "Rachel," Debra bounded over to me, "I had the greatest time! I took a friend along with me. But someone told us to lock our pocketbooks in our car or we would stick out like sore thumbs."

I bet you did anyway, I thought wryly to myself.

"What's that fur hat that some people wear?"

"It's called a *shtreimel*," I replied, smiling.

"And the beanie?"

"We call it a yarmulke," I said, my grin widening.

"And the black hats?"

"We call those black hats."

At that, the entire class, who had been following our exchange, exploded in unreserved mirth.

"And, Rachel, they said they were welcoming the Sabbath bride. Now, how cool is that?"

I nodded. *Yes, it's cool, all right. Very cool.*

"Now listen to this. When services were over, some people invited me and my friend to their house for the Sabbath dinner. Can you believe that? We didn't even know them, and they invited us to come over!"

I wondered who in our shul was so adventurous.

"Now tell me, Rachel, if this isn't the work of G-d. The couple said they're best friends of yours! Their names are Elaine and Chuck. I didn't even tell them I knew you till they asked how I got to your church. When I mentioned your name, they flipped. Isn't that something?!"

"Yes." I was impressed. "That really is something."

"So we went to their house, and it was awesome! Chuck and their guests sang 'A Woman of Valor' to their wives. I told my husband he's gonna have to do the same for me from now on."

Once again, everyone laughed. Then they started teasing Debra about converting to Judaism.

"You know, Rachel, this was some experience. I thought all Jews are from Israel."

"I'm from Philadelphia," I offered, and once again, laughter roared through the room.

A LIFELONG CHALLENGE

ONE MORNING, I was making routine clinical rounds. I knocked and entered a room where a mother sat on the couch, her small baby lying in the crib.

"Good morning," I began. "I'm the chaplain making rounds. My name is Rachel. Is this a good time for you?"

"Sure," she responded with a smile.

"How's this little guy doing?"

The mother proceeded to explain to me about her baby's spina bifida. In his three months of life, he had already endured six surgeries, and she showed me each of the scars. Our conversation continued for twenty minutes, as she explained all of her baby's complicated conditions and the corrective measures that had been taken for each of them.

"He is paralyzed from the waist down," she said in a matter-of-fact way. "That can't be fixed. At least not now; they don't know how. My mother sometimes wonders how I'll manage with him."

Pain encircled me like a tidal wave in an ocean. I looked at the baby, cooing in his crib, and thought, *The little one smiles now, but how will he manage when everyone else is off and running, and he sits on the sidelines and watches? Will he become bitter, or will he use his adversity to become stronger?*

Poor baby...and his poor mother...

"Would you like me to pray?" I asked.

"Please."

"Anything special you want me to include?"

"Just that Andy should lead a long and happy life. And that he should come to terms with his disability and feel happy anyway."

"Master of the Universe, please watch over little Andy and heal him from all of his surgeries. Please allow him to live a long and happy life and to come to peace with his limitations. Allow him to reach his potential, to give You, his parents, and all who know him much joy. Let him inspire others through his determination and fortitude. And please, G-d, give his mother and father lots of strength to handle all of the challenges that they will encounter. For many long, happy, and healthy years. Amen."

"Thank you," she whispered, her eyes shimmering with tears.

I nodded. My eyes swam, too.

"Take care of yourself," I said to Andy's mother. "And you take care of Mommy," I told the baby. He looked straight at me with sweet, innocent eyes.

Oh, Hashem.

SNACK TIME

I WAS ON call at the hospital for a twenty-four-hour shift, starting eight thirty in the morning on Sunday until eight thirty in the morning on Monday. By four o'clock on Sunday afternoon, I found myself rummaging through the cabinets in the chaplain's office in search of a snack.

My eyes lit up as I caught sight of a bag of microwave popcorn. And it was even kosher! I was thrilled.

Hmm, kosher popcorn, *treife* microwave…time to double-wrap. Tying a plastic bag tightly around the bagged popcorn, I set the microwave on the popcorn setting. I waited for popping noises, but they didn't come. No problem, I decided, pressing the popcorn setting once more.

Suddenly, black, smoky spirals began pouring out of the microwave, and I quickly turned it off. *Oh, well,* I thought, staring in dismay at the blackened bag surrounding my popcorn kernels.

I opened the door to wave some of the smoke out, and settled for a grapefruit instead. But it wasn't the same.

About fifteen minutes later, after I'd already closed the door again, I heard a key turning in the lock. *No one's supposed to be here except for me*, I thought, and prickles of apprehension crept up my spine. *Who can that be?*

A swarthy face peered in at me. "I was just about to call security. Everything okay in here?" The cleaning lady looked somewhat alarmed.

"Yes, everything's fine, thanks. Just a little burnt popcorn." I gave a light chuckle.

With a knowing expression, she looked at me. "You know there's a setting for popcorn, don't you?"

Hmm, I thought. *Imagine that.* "Thank you for telling me," I said.

〜♡

GOING HOME EMPTY-HANDED

Is that my pager? I wondered. Someone must have changed the ring; it sounded much too mild. But when I checked it...yup, it was my pager that was buzzing. I sighed. Ready or not...

"A patient is being de-escalated (translation: taken off of life support, or, in our terms, murdered) shortly in CICU (Cardiac Intensive Care Unit). Can you come?"

"I'll be right there," I answered.

I ran. Down the hall, into the elevator, through another hall. When I got to the patient's room, I watched as the baby was passed from his mother to his father and then back again. He was attached to so many wires and appeared listless. Mom rocked him for a while in silence, gazing at him, and then passed him to Dad. Dad rocked the baby and talked to him. He spoke Japanese, but his language was universal. Even I could understand that he was telling his tiny son how much he loved him and all the dreams he'd had for him. Tears poured from his eyes as he spoke in a choked voice. My heart throbbed with his pain.

On the other side of the room, the baby's two-year-old brother and three-year-old sister played happily, coloring pictures and chattering. Every so often, they would run over and show us their pictures, asking our opinion.

And then the nurse asked, "Are you ready?"

Mom nodded. Ever so gently, the tubing was disconnected from the baby. He lay in his mother's arms; Mom looked teary and pained. A few moments passed, and the doctor put his stethoscope on the baby's heart.

"I'm sorry," he said.

There was silence in the room.

"See my picture?" Big sister chirped.

"Sweetie, your baby just went to Heaven," a cousin explained to her. "Where the clouds and stars are."

"That's okay," she answered. "Mommy will get me wings, and I'll go visit him."

My heart contracted with the pure innocence of her comment, and I imagined this little girl soaring Heavenward to visit her brother...

I stayed for two hours, offering an occasional tissue and asking the nurse a question on behalf of the mother. I watched the parents take handprints and footprints of their dead baby, and create molds of his feet to take home. They held him and took pictures. So they wouldn't have to go home empty-handed.

So they wouldn't have to go home empty-handed? My heart

revolted, and nausea rose in my chest. Footprints? Pictures? To replace a—baby?

"Please give me the blanket," Dad asked me, motioning to the crib.

"This one?" I asked, pointing to the white blanket inside the crib.

"Yes. Put it around his feet," he directed softly. "So he won't be cold."

I complied. The baby had died half an hour ago...

Ten weeks prior, shouts of joy had abounded as this baby was placed into his mother's arms for the first time. And now, so soon afterward, there was an abyss of grief and agony as the baby's soul departed from his little body.

We all ride a train through life. Some get off at the first stop, some toward the middle, and some at the end. It all depends on when each passenger has arrived at his or her specific destination. We don't question why some people get off the train earlier than others; as believing Jews, we know they've simply arrived at their destination earlier. But that doesn't mean a person—especially a child's—early demise doesn't leave us with blistering, festering wounds to nurse...

I finally left the hospital and walked into a balmy spring evening outside. The breeze whispered life, while I contemplated death. The flowers smelled redolent, yet I smelled decay. *How can I live life to make it purposeful, Hashem? After all, no one's here forever. You can take me at any time, even momentarily...as it says,* yameinu k'tzeil oveir—*a person's days are like a fleeting shadow.*

I struggled to turn my feelings into a *tefillah. Hashem,* I pleaded, *please wipe the tears from our cheeks. There is so much pain in this world, so much* tza'ar. *Please,* Hakadosh Baruch Hu, *watch over us, protect us, give Klal Yisrael life, give us peace, spare us from all sorrow. Let us live meaningful and joyful lives and make You proud… Please, Hashem, bring Mashiach, and rebuild the Beis Hamikdash, speedily and in our days…*

∿╲╱╲╱╲♡

GRANDMA'S GOLDEN YEARS

DOING ROUNDS IN the hospital always tied my heart in knots. It was something expected of me, yet I always wondered, whenever I entered someone's private hospital room, if the person would have preferred not having his privacy intruded upon.

My first visit of the day was to the room of a toddler. "Good morning," I greeted the older lady who was with the little girl.

"My granddaughter," she explained to me, patting the child's head of golden curls. The toddler was snuggled in bed, and she shifted upon feeling her grandmother's touch.

"That's really nice of you to take a shift," I said, assuming the parents needed a reprieve.

"Oh, I'm with her full-time," Grandma explained. "My daughter can't handle her special needs, so each time Suzie is hospitalized, I come with her."

"Sounds like you've been here a little too much," I ventured.

"Suzie has terrible asthma," Grandma replied. "She can't even play outside, because anything can set off an attack. But sometimes she gets an attack anyway and we have to call 911."

How difficult for a child never to know the joys of playing outdoors!

"You have to manage with what you have," Grandma said, shrugging. "I raised my four children and thought I was done. But then this beauty came along, and I'm like a mother all over again."

"And your daughter?" I ventured.

"Right now, she's in drug rehab," she said, her blue eyes flickering.

Look calm, Rachel. Don't show that you're horrified.

"You're an inspiration," I said. "She's lucky to have you."

And then the dam burst.

"Thank you," she cried. "I just do what I gotta do. But I worry. What if something happens to me? Then who will take care of Suzie? I'm scared."

"That is a scary thought. But with G-d's help, you'll stay healthy for many more years."

"I hope so," she replied.

I left, marveling at how this grandmother's golden years were spent filling in as a full-time mother. She truly was an inspiration.

〜〜〜♡

TUNING INTO ACCEPTANCE

A *FRUM* WOMAN giving a *dvar Torah* to a group of non-Jews. The thought was always somewhat amusing to me, but that was part of my duties as a chaplain: to give some kind of inspirational sermon in the hospital chapel each Wednesday and Sunday. When I asked my *rav* about the permissibility of such a thing—presenting Torah thoughts to non-Jews—he said it was fine so long as I didn't relate any *Torah sheba'al peh* in these sermons. (Thankfully, there were never any issues about what to do in the presence of *avodah zarah* symbols, as there were no religious symbols at all in the hospital chapel.) So I stuck to the *Chumash*, and *baruch Hashem* always managed to come up with something appropriate to say to my listeners.

Striding past the ER one Wednesday, I opened the wooden

door of the chapel and entered the room, only to find a black woman *shuckling* over her version of Tehillim right in the front, at the lectern, where I was supposed to stand for my sermon.

Hmm, I can't chase her away. Boy, she's really having a lot of ka-vanah; I don't want to disturb her. But I'm supposed to start at seven, and the time is now… What do I do?

Feeling my gaze on her, the woman finally turned around. When she saw me, she smiled and then walked to the back of the room.

I took my place at the lectern and started to wax dramatic. The woman looked at me, surprised. *Why, it's just the two of us,* I could see her thinking, a question mark dangling in her eyes.

"Patients and families can tune in from their rooms," I explained. "So even though this looks like an empty room, we may have countless spectators. On the other hand," I added with an irrepressible grin, "we may have none. Who knows?" I shrugged and continued.

That evening I brought lessons on acceptance of *ratzon Hashem* from *Parshas Shemini*, relaying how Aharon was silent when Nadav and Avihu met their deaths. I talked about Dovid Hamelech, who, when fleeing from Avshalom, calmly accepted Shimi ben Geira's curses without any desire for retaliation.

Then I described Moshe's prayerful entreaties to be granted entry into Eretz Yisrael, and our *Imahos* storming the Heavens until Hashem granted them children.

"So you see," I concluded, "the Bible enjoins us to accept what we cannot change. We must align our will with G-d's. However, when there is hope—and whenever there's life, there's always hope—we must pray with all our strength. G-d wants our closeness; He wants a relationship, and prayer helps."

I concluded the service with a few translated *perakim* of Tehillim from my Hebrew-English edition.

"I really enjoyed that," my audience of one told me. She then shared that she was here in the hospital with her baby granddaughter, who would stop breathing every time she lay on her back.

"Thank you for your kind words," I said, "and I hope your granddaughter has a speedy recovery. Would you like me to pray for her?"

She nodded, and we prayed for her baby granddaughter's recovery together.

ㅗㅆㅗㅆ♡

SAVING GOODBYE

BEEP, BEEP, BEEP.

The spoonful of chili was in my hand, and my mouth was open to receive it. Down went the spoon as I reached for my pager.

"This is Rachel from the chaplain's office. Can I help you?"

"We have a critically ill patient here in PICU (Pediatric Intensive Care Unit)," the nurse explained. "Mom wants a chaplain."

"I'll be right up."

I took two minutes to finish the chili before it got cold. The salad would wait.

I knocked and entered the patient's room. It was a baby girl who was very sick.

"They told us," Mom said in a choked voice, "they told us that she probably won't make it through the night."

"I'm so sorry," I said. "I'm so very, very sorry." And I held the mother while she cried.

"Pray for her," she asked me. "Please."

"What would you like me to pray for?" I wondered if she were asking me to pray for a miracle.

"Pray that she live through the night. Pray for life."

I came close to the little bassinet where the baby's chest was rising up and down rapidly. I stroked her little feet and arms. I didn't like the color of her face; it was almost gray. Despite my feelings that she was not going to remain with us for long, I asked Hashem to send her a *refuah sheleimah*, that she live for many, many more long, healthy, and happy years.

But Hakadosh Baruch Hu, I added silently, *if Your answer is no, please give the mother the strength to get through this ordeal.*

An hour later, I got the call. The baby had passed away.

I watched the distraught parents, two beautiful sisters, two aunts, and a grandmother dissolve in heartbroken grief. The baby was passed from one set of arms to another, as each family member bid her a tender goodbye, rocked her, and kissed her. She looked like an angel now, her coloring suddenly normal. But her eyes were closed, and her heartbeat was still.

"How long can I hold her?" Mom asked the nurse.

"As long as you want," the nurse said.

"You mean forever?" The mother lifted her tearstained face, and my eyes met hers. She had voiced my own immediate thought, because how, indeed, can parents say goodbye to their child?

I walked out. I had to cry.

CRAISINS FOR A PEACE OFFERING

"RACHEL?" IT WAS Joan, my supervisor, calling me.

"Yes?"

"Please come into my office."

Uh-oh, what did I do to deserve an unscheduled meeting with her?

"Were you with the family whose child passed away last night?"

"Yes."

"Where is the death certificate?"

"It wasn't ready, so I figured I could pick it up today."

Joan shook her head and folded her arms across her chest, radiating disapproval. "That must be done immediately. Our records are critical. Not to mention the fact that if something isn't documented, it's as if it didn't happen."

Raising my eyebrows, I pondered that for a moment. I was there; it had definitely happened.

I agree that records are important. But didn't it matter that I was with the family for hours throughout the night? Why was I only called in when something wasn't perfect, while all of the efforts that I *did* put in seemed to go unrecognized? In spite of my efforts to look impassive, my eyes filled.

"I'll take care of it," I said softly. "But I did stay with them for a long time."

I was dismissed with a curt nod.

"What happened?" Dayna, another chaplain student, asked with concern, seeing my face. I filled her in, expressing my frustration with the system.

While we sat at our computers, recording our chaplaincy visits, I heard my name being called. Turning around, I saw Joan, her lips curved in a slight smile.

"Rachel, I was putting out some snacks, and I wanted to know if these were kosher."

I picked up the package of Craisins she held out, nodded, and thanked her for thinking of me.

"That was her way of making up," Dayna whispered, putting a hand on my shoulder.

"Yeah, I kind of figured as much."

AN OPPORTUNITY FOR *KIDDUSH HASHEM*

"Rachel," Dayna said to me one day, "I'm doing a research paper on Judaism for one of my classes. I wondered if we could meet for lunch and I could interview you."

"Of course." There was no way I could say no. Dayna had helped me so many times as I struggled to navigate the complicated web of the hospital computer system.

So we met at a kosher eatery for lunch, and I wondered what people thought as I came in accompanied by this six-foot-tall, blonde-haired woman in jeans. Over sandwiches, I tried explaining the laws that govern a Jew's everyday life. She listened intently.

"Tell me about your Sabbath," she asked, and I tried to describe in words our weekly island of serenity. When I finished, taking her from Erev Shabbos preparations to the *seudos* and the atmosphere of the holy day itself, her eyes glowed with respect and admiration.

"We don't have anything like that," she marveled. "That's so beautiful."

When I walked back to my car and drove off, I hoped I had made a *kiddush Hashem*.

FROM ONE MOMENT TO THE NEXT...

"A five-year-old child just went into cardiac arrest," the

nurse informed me when I answered the call. "She was airlifted and we've been working on her for a while. The child's mother just arrived; please go and be there for her."

The child had been frolicking on the grass, picking flowers and playing with a friend under a neighbor's watchful eye; Mom was away at the dentist. The neighbor was startled when suddenly, the child's friend came over and began pulling on his arm.

"Lisa's sleeping," the friend said.

"Sleeping?!" the neighbor exclaimed, glancing in alarm at the prone figure on the lawn. "That's impossible; she was just up and playing a minute ago!"

The neighbor ran to Lisa and immediately began CPR, while his wife called 911. And here they were at the hospital now, Lisa being worked on, the neighbor looking like he was in a state of shock, and Mom shedding copious tears.

"Please," Mom begged every nurse who came in to update her. "Please make sure her yellow ducky is near her ear. If she wakes up and doesn't see her ducky right away, she'll be very upset."

Lisa was intubated and put on ECMO, technical machinery that would help her heart and lungs continue to work. I sat with Mom for a while, and a loud silence filled the room. I finally told her I would return and check on her later.

But later the situation remained grim.

One moment a child is healthy, playing, laughing, carefree. The next moment, life is turned upside-down, as she fights for life in the ICU. But her ducky rests beside her now for when she wakes up—oh, Hashem, may she please wake up...

After this encounter, I resolved to say *Asher Yatzar*, the blessing in which we thank Hashem for our health, with more *kavanah*, especially while doing my work in the hospital. Health is not something that can ever be taken for granted.

THE INTRUDER

THE NOISE OF a key being inserted into the lock grabbed my attention, and my eyes flew open. I had been sleeping fitfully in the chaplaincy sleep room, and no one was supposed to be in the office other than me. My heart began pounding wildly, and I wondered who was coming in at five o'clock in the morning. Fear slithered up and down my spine, and I felt very vulnerable and alone.

Suddenly I heard loud hammering and ripping noises, and my temperature began to rise.

You've got to be kidding! A worker at FIVE in the morning?! While a defenseless woman is sleeping in the next room? No way!

Donning regular clothes and my *sheitel*, I marched out and glared at this man, standing on a ladder with his head inside the dropped ceiling.

"What are you doing here?" I asked, my words dripping venom.

"Fixin' the leak."

"Didn't you see the sign on the door that says to page the chaplain if you need something? These are not normal working hours."

"Oh, I'm sorry, Chaplain, I didn't mean to disturb you."

"Well, you did. Please go out now."

The poor handyman gathered his tools and left on the double, looking like he wasn't sure what hit him. I felt a twinge of remorse, but what was he thinking? Five a.m.?!

Then more guilt assailed me as I wondered if I had made a *chillul Hashem*. Who said chaplains, especially Jewish ones, are allowed to get angry?

CHAPLAIN INDICTED FOR PRAYING

"Who's on call tonight? Who's on call? Hello?" A familiar sing-song voice bursts into the office after hours. The voice is insistent, demanding an answer.

Well, I'm on call, but I'm also mid-*Shemoneh Esrei*, and I can't answer the staff chaplain right now.

As a result of my failure to answer that call, I got a reprimanding email from my supervisor telling me that I must be available to receive reports from the staff chaplain when I come on call at four thirty each day.

"But I was!" I protested. "This was already after five, and all I was doing was praying my afternoon service, which doesn't take longer than ten minutes. I didn't even know anyone was still here and that there was any crisis going on. Anyone could be unavailable for ten minutes—a person could be in the shower, bathroom, cafeteria…"

Well, we worked it out. I explained what happened to the staff chaplain and to my supervisor, and they accepted my justification. But I was highly offended. I thought chaplains were socially adept. Why hadn't the staff chaplain simply come and talked to me about her supposed grievance? She had to report me to my supervisor?

"Why are you so upset, Rachel?" my supervisor asked, trying to understand.

"It's twofold," I told her. "One, when I have an issue with someone, I always approach them directly first. If I can't resolve the issue, then I approach a third party. But I think it's wrong and inconsiderate to report someone to her supervisor without first trying to have direct communication with her.

"Second," I continued, as a memory of flashing blue lights suddenly surfaced in my mind, "it's just like the time when I got a ticket for not stopping at a stop sign—when I *know* I *had* stopped. I was indignant, and actually went to court to fight it. I did stop. Of course I stopped! If I had received a speeding ticket while going over the speed limit, I could have accepted that. But to get a ticket for something I didn't do—that tasted bitter."

"Injustice," my supervisor said, nodding sagely.

"Yes," I said, feeling somewhat better. At least she understood.

Later, as I rehashed the episode in my mind once more, I imagined bold, glaring headlines with the eye-catching caption: "Chaplain Indicted for Praying While on Call at the Hospital." Sounds somewhat like a contradiction in terms. Oh, well. This is all a learning experience. But considering the superhuman effort I was exerting and the sacrifices I was making to fulfill the program requirements, I allowed myself to lick my wounds.

BONDING WITH GRANDMA

A FOUR-YEAR-OLD GIRL passed away right before I went on call. I was glad I missed it. But then...

"Rachel, the grandmother of that girl is having pain, so she was brought to the ER. Please go to her and see how she's doing."

"Okay." I set off toward the ER.

Grandma lay on the stretcher, moaning and rubbing her abdomen.

"I'm so sorry for your loss," I said as I came close to her. "I'm the chaplain on call now; my name is Rachel."

"Thank you," she whispered, her eyes glittering with tears.

Nurses and doctors came in and out of the room, and Grandma and I bonded. She showed me pictures of her little granddaughter from today and yesterday. The realization that this girl was no longer alive stunned me; she looked so alive in the pictures. Just a moment ago she was here, and now she was gone... Life is so short, so transient, so very precious.

Grandma cried on me. Then she began telling me a little about her life. We discovered we were *landsleit*, both hailing from Philadelphia, and that increased our sense of connection.

Discovering our common roots set a flood of memories in motion for me. I thought of my hometown, and my mother, who had passed away almost eighteen years ago. I remember calling my home number in Philadelphia after she died, willing her to answer, even though I knew she was no longer in this world.

I pictured the house of my childhood and my rural neighborhood. I hadn't thought of it in so long... There was the red maple tree that stood in our front yard. Was it still alive? It had to be; it had weathered every storm of my childhood, and besides, it was part of my memories. All of these nostalgic thoughts zipped through my mind as I listened to Grandma speak about her own Philadelphia memories.

Then the EMS team came to wheel Grandma, who felt like my good friend at this point, into their van and transport her to an adult hospital, since, as the doctor bluntly said, "We don't treat us old folks here, y'know. This is a children's hospital."

I said goodbye to Grandma and asked if I could give her a hug for the road. She melted into my arms and said, "I wish I could see you again. I wish you'd come to Philadelphia."

"Me, too..." I smiled wistfully. "Me, too."

I escorted her a few steps down the hall before returning to the office.

One of the more difficult parts of this job seemed to be forming incredibly intimate bonds with people, born from crisis situations, and then, as suddenly as they'd enter my life, they'd leave. And I'd never see or hear from them again, they'd become like a wisp, a dream.

Perhaps the concept could be seen as a microcosm of life in this world, with every encounter like another scene from a play, and after each scene, the curtains fall. And then it's time to move on, step forward, and not look back. Yet each scene in the play is dependent on the former one for the story to unfold.

In life, we are the cast in a major production. Each encounter we have, each action we do, is another scene in the story of our life. When the curtains fall for the last time, after one hundred and twenty years, with Hashem's help, we hope the Director will be pleased with His handiwork, that He'll smile at His cast and tell us, "Well done!"

JUMPING THE FENCE

THIS SCENE COULD have come from a horror novel, but unfortunately, it was all too real…

A hysterical mother walked alongside her little boy's stretcher, crying and shaking. And finally, through her tears, the story of what had happened emerged.

She had little Alex strapped into his stroller in the parking lot of a playground. A van was heading her way, and a police car was following hot on its tail, blue lights flashing in warning.

That van is not going to jump the fence, is it? the mother thought to herself, watching the scene and the fence that separated her from the van, but she hadn't even finished the thought when suddenly, her fears materialized before her very eyes. Driving right through the fence, the van careened into her stroller, sending her little one flying onto the asphalt!

Thank G-d, all little Alex suffered were some relatively minor abrasions on his lip and a hematoma on his head; there was no internal damage. To the mother's immense relief, the medical team reassured her that her little guy was going to be fine.

But, oh my goodness! A stolen van (as it was later discovered to be), driven by some criminals trying to outrun the police, crashing into a baby in his stroller... Whoever coined the line "Truth is stranger than fiction" must have been a chaplain!

ALL IN A NIGHT'S WORK

I WAS DOING my best to comfort a distraught mother whose child was in a car accident. She had been told that he would probably not make it.

"Don't go," the mother pleaded with him, sobbing, holding his hand. "If you go, I go with you. You are my life. Don't go..."

Tears streamed down my cheeks as I held her and tried to just be with her in her pain. And then I found out that part of her grief was not grief at all, but actually guilt; she had given up her son to foster care, and had not been with him for the last five years other than for occasional visitation.

"You were my life," she sobbed, while the foster mother, at the boy's bedside, too, rolled her eyes.

"I don't know what she's going on about," she told me. "I'm the one who's been with him since he was five. She gave him up, said she didn't want him..."

Appearances can certainly be deceiving. Who would have imagined? The power of guilt...

LATER THAT EVENING—it was already midnight—I was on my couch-bed when the pager sounded its strident alarm.

"Chaplaincy," I said, returning the call.

"Can you bring up a bible to room 4125, please?"

"Now?" I asked, incredulous.

The question was rhetorical. If the patient had been okay with waiting until morning, the nurse wouldn't have paged me now. So on came my work clothes and *sheitel*, and up I went to room 4125. I wondered if people realize that chaplains also like to sleep at night.

FOUR IN THE morning.

"Code blue, code blue!"

I jumped up and began throwing on my clothes again. When there's a code blue emergency call, a chaplain's got to *run* to the scene.

Midway, another announcement came on: "Code blue, canceled. Code blue, canceled."

I sighed and got back into "bed." All in a night's work.

OH, FOR A HEALTHY KIDNEY...

I WAS ASKED to go up to cardiac intensive care to visit with the family of a very sick baby, and the tears remained on my face long after the visit was over. A six-day-old baby. I came up and saw the young mother crying next to the baby's crib. Grandma, the mother's mother, stood close by. She was also crying. Tubes threaded in and out of this baby's tiny body, while a respirator pushed air into his lungs.

"They say he may not make it. He's so sick," Mom told me while I massaged her shoulder. "It hurts so much. He's so little. Why? Why did I have to have him if he was just going to be taken from me?"

I had no words. I did my best to communicate support and empathy by standing nearby, listening, and gently massaging the mother.

"Why is G-d punishing me?" she burst out.

"Please," I protested. "It doesn't have to mean that G-d is punishing you, although this is so very, very difficult, so painful. There's a purpose for every soul that G-d brings into this world, and we don't understand—we don't understand anything. It's like we're riding a bus, taking a trip. Some people get off at the first stop, some at the second, and some wait until the very end. Why? Why does everyone get off at different points? Because each person has his own destination…"

"Yes," she said. "That makes sense."

Grandma was quietly sobbing and wiping her eyes. The doctor came to speak with us. His face was solemn.

"It's nice to meet you," he began, "although I'm sorry that it's under these circumstances. You know your baby's very sick. He has a serious heart problem, but right now he's also got a bacterial infection in his kidneys that his body is having a hard time fighting. If his body can manage to start producing urine within the next twelve hours, then maybe, hopefully, he'll be able to gain a bit more strength and then we can do the heart surgery that he needs. But in his state right now, he wouldn't be able to withstand the heart surgery.

"If he does not begin to produce urine within the next twelve hours, well, then, he may just deteriorate until...until he dies."

The mother and grandmother's tears flowed unchecked.

"Let's wait and see what happens," the doctor continued. "I hope you two can go home and get some sleep. Hopefully the baby will have an uneventful night..." He wished them well and then left.

Mom walked over to the crib and spoke to little Nathan. "You need to get well," she told him, holding his tiny fingers in hers. "But if it's your time, it's okay. You can go home to G-d..."

I went over to Grandma, and she fell into my embrace.

"Twenty-three years ago, I lost a child," she whispered. "I went to the hospital to have a baby, and I came home without one. He never came home. He had a bad heart. And now I'm seeing it again in my grandson..."

I held her while she cried. Our tears mingled, flowing freely. I walked them into the elevator and wished them a good night. When the doors opened on the first floor, Mom grabbed my arm.

"Can you pray for us?" she pleaded.

"Of course."

A cheerful black cleaning lady passed by, saw us holding hands, and ran over to us.

"Can I join y'all and pray with you?" she asked.

In different circumstances, I would have laughed out loud; now, I sufficed with a chuckle deep inside. The cleaning lady held Mom and Grandma's hands, and the four of us stood there together, a group of strangers, united in prayer, united in caring.

"May it be Your will, G-d," I prayed, "that You bring healing to little Nathan. Strengthen his body, and allow the doctors to be able to treat his illness, and to do so successfully. Our Father, we ask You, we beg You, for Nathan's recovery. But Master of the World, if Your answer is no, please give Nathan's mother and grandmother the strength to handle Your decision. We trust You, and we know You will do what's best. Please, Almighty G-d, protect Nathan and his family, and let them feel Your love."

"Amen," the others answered in one voice. Then each of them gave me a hug.

I walked slowly toward my office, head down, tears flowing. I thought my well of tears had run dry by then, but I guess it hadn't, because my eyes kept streaming.

Health is such a gift. Here was a tiny baby, hanging onto life by a thread, because of his malfunctioning kidneys... Did *I* fully appreciate *my* thankfully working kidneys?

I thought about a young man in our community who, just two years ago, had been fighting for his life, also due to kidney failure. Then one day, he received the ultimate gift—the gift of life—in the form of a new kidney. I will never forget his wife's words after he got that new kidney.

"He has a working kidney. A real, live, working kidney!" she cried.

And we, who *baruch Hashem* have *two* "real, live, working kidneys"...well, what can *we* say?

At the very least, we should appreciate the tremendous gift of health we've been granted, and never stop thanking Hashem for it...

Baruch Atah Hashem, Rofei chol basar u'mafli la'asos—Blessed are You, Hashem, Healer of all flesh, Who performs wonders.

PRAYER POWER

A six-year-old just diagnosed with a brain tumor? Ribono Shel Olam, *what do I say?*

I strode upstairs, asking Hashem to put the right words in my mouth.

Mom was trembling violently, and nurses were easing her into a wheelchair. Doctors and nurses escorted her into a small consult room where she could lie down on a couch. She began to breathe deeply and became totally unresponsive. Repeated efforts were made to communicate with her, but to no avail. Her own mother, the sick child's grandmother, came running in and tried speaking to her, but her eyes remained closed, and she did not speak or react.

I held Mom's hand, alternately speaking to her and to her mother.

"I'm so sorry about the diagnosis," I whispered.

"You gotta be strong for Riley," Grandma urged. "There's plenty to be hopeful about. If it didn't spread, there's a lot they can do."

Silence. No response.

I had never before witnessed a person in shock. I couldn't figure out if Mom was intentionally shutting us out of her world because she didn't want to speak, or if this was her body's reaction to the shock and she really was unable to speak or even make eye contact.

We offered drinks, food, made jokes.

After an hour and a half, I didn't know what else to do for this mother. I found myself wishing she would just snap out of it. *Get a hold of yourself!* I felt like shouting at her. *Your daughter needs you! If you're hospitalized now, what will happen when your little girl calls for Mommy? And where should Daddy go, to be with you or his little girl? Come on, Mom, wake up and go take care of your daughter.*

"Would it be okay with you if I pray?" I finally asked. Grandma nodded.

"And I hope it's okay with you, too, Heather," I said to Mom. Silence.

I *davened* for the child's full recovery, for the doctors to have the required wisdom to treat her illness. I *davened* that the family should have strength while going through this trying ordeal.

As I *davened*, never letting go of Heather's hand, she began to shake again, and tears coursed down her cheeks. Within moments of my conclusion, she opened her eyes.

"Room," she said in a muffled voice.

Grandma and I struggled to understand her; the word she had said was garbled, as if surrounded by a thick fog. At last, we understood, and our eyes danced with excitement; she wanted to go back to Riley!

Grandma and I helped her walk back to her daughter's hospital room.

Baruch Hashem! I marveled. The power of prayer…

IN THE BOXING RING

During our Monday group session, my fellow chaplain trainees and I sat around the table and discussed the barriers and fears we have that might impede our performances. One intern mentioned that his youth was an impediment; he felt no one would respect him because, "What could I know? I mean, really, what life experience can I possibly have at my age?"

Almost everyone reassured him that people don't necessarily

look at a person's age; rather, they judge him by his presence. I wasn't sure I agreed; I myself was familiar with the feeling of smug superiority when faced with a very young professional telling me something. *Who is he/she to tell this to me?* I've wondered. *I could be his/her mother!*

"Don't worry," I quipped. "I guarantee, this is one impediment that *will* change."

Laughter filled the room, and everyone nodded.

I silently acknowledged one of my own fears: what would the families I comfort say if they knew I was Jewish? Most often, the issue doesn't come up at all. But just recently, Hashem tossed me a curve ball, and I had a very interesting encounter…

"GOOD MORNING," I said, knocking and entering a room with a smile. "My name is Rachel. I'm the chaplain coming to see how you're doing."

"I'm Bob, this is my wife, Cindy, and this here is my sister and brother-in-law, Grace and Mark. Pleased to meet you."

I nodded. "Same here."

"So," Bob drawled, "what church do you go to?"

"Well," I ventured, my heart in my throat, "I'm Jewish, so I don't go to church; I attend a synagogue instead."

"You're Jewish?" Bob echoed. "And you go to all people?"

I nodded. "Yes."

He took a heavy breath. "Even Moslems, Hindus…?"

"Yes," I repeated. "We cater to everyone."

"But how do you do that?" he countered. "I mean, isn't that a conflict for you?"

"We focus on commonality, not differences," I answered,

davening fervently for the right words. "We all have a G-d Who takes care of us and watches over us, right?"

"Well," Bob declared, "I think that's wrong. If you believe in a certain religion, you should be trying to convert 'em all to that religion."

I smiled sweetly. "That's not my job."

"Oh, yes, it is," he retorted. "And in my opinion, everyone should believe in J.C."

Hmm, hmm, hmm. You don't say...

"You're entitled to your opinion," I assured him, while feeling he really wasn't—not *that* opinion, anyway. "I hope your child has a speedy recovery and a return to good health, and that G-d answers all of your prayers." *About your child, that is, not about your belief system.*

I'm no boxer, but I felt as if I had just fought my first boxing match with an opponent who was trying his utmost to flatten me. I was anxious to leave before round two could start. Turning toward the door, I could almost smell the freedom I knew awaited me on the other side.

"Take care," I said.

"Thank you," Bob's wife said, and I bolted.

After an encounter like that, I would not have risked returning to the line of fire. But one week later, I actually marched right into that same room while doing my rounds. I had been up the entire night before while on call and, in my exhausted state, I'd simply forgotten just whose room it was.

"I remember you," the patient's mother greeted me with a smile.

"Oh," I said with a smile, trying to play along while racking my memory. *Who was this patient?* "How are you?"

She explained that they really should have been discharged a few days ago, but glitches kept coming up. "But I'm very grateful that Adam seems to have turned a corner now and is doing much better."

"Oh, good, I'm glad to hear that," I said.

"You know, my husband isn't always like that," she shared.

And it all came flooding back. Her husband was Bob, the man who had tried to start up with my Judaism! Oh, no, I wasn't ready for any more of that. My heart started hammering violently, and I wanted to escape before the heat came on in the form of her husband. Was he somewhere in the hospital? Oh, please, I hope not...

"Yeah...I figured things were just...really hard for him. Your son was in surgery, after all... Don't worry, I didn't take it personally." *If you believe that, lady, you'll believe anything.*

"Well, he's also going through some of his own health challenges. He finally got an appointment with a certain specialist after months of waiting; that's why he's not here today."

I am so glad he's not. I hope his appointment takes a good, long time.

"So, what kind of Jew are you?" Bob's wife asked me conversationally.

What a powerful question, especially considering that it's right before Rosh Hashanah. What kind of Jew am I, indeed?

"I mean," she clarified, "are you a Christian Jew or an Orthodox Jew?"

Inwardly shuddering, I answered that I belong to the latter category.

"You know, I really find it very interesting, different people and different religions and all that. But I don't want to embarrass you with a lot of questions."

"Oh, no, it's fine. I'm very open, and I'm used to questions."

That didn't elicit much of a response, and so I decided to wrap up the conversation. "Well, I wish Adam a speedy recovery, and I hope things start looking up for you."

"Thank you, Chaplain," she replied. "We have a lot of people praying for us, all over. Would you pray for Adam, too?"

Something in her manner made me ask, "Now? Or in private?"

"Privately, please. Adam wants to rest now. We would really appreciate that."

"I certainly will. All the best to you." I smiled and left.

Once I was back out in the hall, I felt glad that I had walked into the room. At least we had some type of closure here, ending on a positive note.

BARRING ENTRY TO THE PROMISED LAND

"THE COUPLE HAD waited seven years for a child, struggling through the bottomless pain of infertility, only to have their long-awaited child diagnosed with a brain tumor at age two." A fellow chaplain-in-training related the story of her recent encounter, while we, her peers, sat and listened.

"Months of harrowing treatments passed, and the child succumbed to her illness. I was called in to console them."

Through her tears, she related the conversation she'd had with the couple, in which she'd shared with them her own personal struggle with infertility. And she said the following words that resonated and touched me deeply.

"To wait seven years for a child, only to have the child snatched away, reminds me of what happened to Moses. After forty years of guiding the Jewish nation selflessly and devotedly, he was told to ascend the mountain top where he would see the Promised Land, but he would not be permitted to enter there.

"In the same way, these parents had their child, but were not permitted to bring her to adulthood; they saw her, but were not allowed to enter the Promised Land."

My eyes filled as I listened to this young woman, touching her own grief as she attempted to console a young couple. I, too, knew people struggling with infertility, and I could deeply empathize with the searing pain of unfulfilled dreams.

"May G-d answer your prayers," I whispered to my classmate afterward, encircling her with a strong embrace. *All of our prayers*, I added silently.

CODE BLUE!

A DAY LATER, I was the one in need of a strong embrace, but there was no one around to give it to me. I was summoned to the NICU (Neonatal Intensive Care Unit) for two babies, both of whom were expected to die imminently.

Taking a deep breath, I entered the first curtained cubicle. Inside were the baby's parents and a grandmother, all of them weeping copiously.

The mother held the baby in her arms. "It's okay, Andre," she soothed him. "It's gonna be okay, y'hear me? You're a fighter; you're my baby boy. It's gonna be okay, y'hear me?"

Dad began to shake and weep convulsively.

"Hey, Allen, don't you fall apart now. I need you to be strong. There's a reason for all this, you hear me? There's a reason."

"I've lost all my faith," Dad cried.

"No!" Mom shouted. "Don't do that! You've gotta be strong, for me, for Andre."

Dad nodded, crying.

"It's okay to let out the pain," I whispered to him. "It's okay—whatever you're feeling right now is okay."

Once Dad calmed down, Mom switched gears. "No, no, no," she chanted. "No, not my baby boy. No, you can't go. You're my baby. How will I live without you? Andre, you're a fighter. Please, Andre… G-d, please, please, no, no, no…"

The raw pain was overwhelming. I held Mom's shoulder, rubbing and caressing her.

The baby made eye contact with his mother.

"I see you, Andre," she cooed. "I see you looking at me. And I'm gonna see you again. We're all gonna see you again, up in Heaven, y'hear? You're not alone…"

"He's talking to you," I murmured. "He's telling you he loves you."

Finally, the baby passed away. This tiny, pure human being appeared to be sleeping, but we knew he would not wake up. While Mom, Dad, and the extended family surrounded the crib, Dad began to shake. Suddenly he fainted, and quiet grief became bedlam.

"Code blue!" one nurse shouted. "Push the button!"

"He's having a seizure," Mom explained. "He's epileptic, and he didn't take his medicine. Allen, I told you, calm down. It's gonna be okay."

The room filled with nurses and medical technicians. Dad was hoisted onto a stretcher, an oxygen mask affixed to his face, and wheeled down to the emergency room. We all looked at each other in shock—could things get any worse?

They could.

"Chaplain," a nurse whispered in my ear, "there's another baby just a few doors down. She's dying, and I think they might need you in there."

Oh, no. This was too much…

Off I went. The family was mostly Spanish speaking, though they understood who I was and accepted my condolences. Mom allowed me to give her a hug.

As I entered each room and saw these tiny souls whose lives had been snuffed out, I felt Hashem. His Presence was so strong, so powerful. For who else holds the keys to life and death?

I felt You there, Hashem, just as I felt the pain as You gathered these little souls back to You…

╼╫╾╫╾♡

WITH US IN THE GOOD TIMES AND THE BAD…

THE NEXT MORNING, before I started my routine visits, I felt that I needed a break after the intensity of the night before. I went to a little park just down the road and walked down the scenic path which encircled a small lake, gathering momentum as I moved.

Was I trying to leave death behind? Perhaps.

The air was cool, brisk and refreshing. I drank great gulps of the invigorating cocktail, reveling in feeling alive, while continuing to grieve and mourn the deaths from the night before.

Great bursts of sunlight streamed onto the lake in shimmering gold. A beautiful blue heron stood majestically in the depths, a silent testimony to our Creator's wisdom and grandeur. And again, I suddenly felt Hashem's Presence, as if He were a finger's reach away. I marveled at that heron and at the beautiful scene spread out in front of me, and wordlessly thanked Hashem for giving me another day of glorious life.

When I returned to the chaplain office, I found another chaplain trainee there. I was glad; I needed to talk. I told her about my encounters the night before. Then I told her about the beautiful heron and the nature scene I'd seen that morning.

"Both times I sensed G-d's closeness," I said. "Last night, He was there with us in death. And today, there He was, in the sunlight and live beauty. Such stark, contrasting situations…"

My peer nodded and let me talk. Then she gave me a hug. In it, I found compassion and understanding. As a fellow chaplain-in-training, she'd gone through similar encounters. She knew exactly how I felt.

Hashem is truly with us always, both in the good times and the times that, to us, may seem bad. What was so moving to me was the degree of closeness to Him that I actually felt, both during the difficult experiences of the night before and during the glorious morning today.

-∿-∿-♡

A WELCOME BREAK FROM THE CHAPLAIN'S BADGE

My son was getting married out of town. The night before I was to travel for the wedding, I was on call. Hashem gave me a gift: for the first time ever, the pager did not go off even once. I was astounded and profoundly grateful; I really didn't feel up to dealing with others when my emotions were on that mother-of-the-*chassan* roller coaster. A miracle? Perhaps.

A week after the *chasunah*, I returned to the hospital to do clinical rounds. My feet were not totally back on the ground yet. The last *sheva brachos* had just been the night before in our city, and the *chassan* and *kallah* were due to be at the airport, flying to their new home, that afternoon. I wished I could be with them, and not in the hospital, during their last few hours in town.

I walked into a room where a bright-eyed, golden-haired child was sitting up in her bed; there was no one else in the room.

"Hi there," I said. "I came to visit you."

"What's your name?" she chirped in a bouncy kind of way.

"Rachel." I smiled, entranced. "What's yours?"

"Katie," she replied. "My mommy's at a class. What's your favorite animal?"

This is fun, I thought, pulling up a chair to sit beside her bed. We discussed favorite animals and favorite colors, and she showed me a necklace that her mommy made for her. When breakfast was delivered, I spread cream cheese on her bagel and opened her purple freeze-pop (purple was her favorite color).

It was fun to discard the chaplain badge and just act like the Jewish mother I am and love to be.

ENDLESS TEARS

As I CAME on call for a twenty-four-hour shift, I reluctantly took the beeper from my colleague's outstretched hand. Okay, I'll admit it; I was a little burned out. So for all of you chaplain trainees out there, don't listen to this part, because negativity can be contagious.

I was just tired, tired of leaving my family at dinner and bed-time, tired of having to say goodbye to my five-year-old on a Sunday morning, knowing that I wouldn't see her again until Monday afternoon.

"Mommy," she said to me the night before, snuggled against me on the couch, "I won't let you leave. Don't leave me ever again, 'kay?"

"Oh, Tehila, I wish I wouldn't have to! But soon, my darling, soon this part of the program will be all over. And then I won't have to leave at night anymore."

So I walked into the office with a heavy heart, hoping that at least the day wouldn't be too hectic.

Ten minutes into those hopes, the beeper went off. Off I zoomed to the emergency room, where I witnessed CPR in action. A three-month-old baby lay on the table, and a nurse was administering CPR. The baby had gone into sudden cardiac arrest, and the medical team was desperately trying to revive her.

"Anyone who can relieve her?" a doctor called out, while the rest of us in the room stood like silent sentinels, watching, hoping, praying.

A different nurse smoothly transitioned into the first one's position and began to work strenuously.

"How long has it been?" the doctor's voice rang out.

"Twenty minutes while we took her over here," an EMS worker replied.

"And how long in here?" the doctor wanted to know.

"About twenty minutes."

"We'll give it five more minutes," the doctor announced impassively.

And if it were your daughter? I wondered uncharitably. *Is it ever enough tries when it comes to saving a life?*

Five minutes passed. No change, no heartbeat.

"Stop," the doctor ordered.

I saw everyone's faces fall. The nurses, the EMS technicians—everyone had hoped for a different outcome. But it was not to be.

The child's family had not yet arrived, so I left, asking to be paged once they came. Mom finally came after what felt like a long time, and a doctor, nurse, social worker, and I escorted her into a consult room. There she was told that her baby was gone.

I enfolded Mom in my arms while she cried. I had nothing else to give her.

WAITING AND WORRYING

I WAS DOING clinical rounds, and I went to visit the mother of a little baby.

"How are you?" I asked, introducing myself.

"Oh, I'm okay," she said, and then began to cry.

"I don't know what's wrong with me," she apologized. "I'm so hormonal."

"That's okay," I said.

"It's just that he's had this infection, and he was really unresponsive. But they think the medicine is starting to kick in now. He's eating; that's a good sign."

We talked for a while. When she asked me what church I was with, I thought, *Oh no, here we go again.*

"Well," I said with a smile, "I'm actually not with any church. I'm Jewish."

"Oh! That's nice," she replied, not seeming shocked or horrified in the least bit. "And what temple are you with?"

We continued to talk a little more, and finally, she thanked me for coming. She seemed like the warm, fuzzy type, so I asked if I could give her a hug.

"Sure." She smiled, and I embraced her.

"Wow, that had so much love," she said. "Thank you so much."

"You take care." I patted her shoulder. "Hope everything gets much better."

And I left and closed the door.

Further down the hall, I entered a room, and a young couple

looked at me with anxious eyes.

"Failure to thrive," Mom explained the baby's condition. "He's a month old and isn't gaining weight. And the doctors can't figure out why. It's just so hard waiting for a diagnosis."

"Waiting and worrying," I murmured. "Well, I hope that the doctors are able to diagnose the condition very soon, and that it's one that can be easily remedied. And I wish your baby a full recovery."

"Thank you so much," both parents said.

That "waiting and worrying" period, while medical tests are conducted and doctors are struggling to figure out what is wrong with the patient, is so taxing. I've heard it said that this period is actually the optimal time for *tefillah*, as before a *gezeirah* is concrete, there's more of a chance for it to still be changed.

AN OPEN HEART

Tinsel-covered doors, larger-than-life X-mas trees, music playing season-related songs, and, wherever I looked, pictures of an old man with a white beard and red coat, matching hat, and flushed cheeks… In my own personal *galus* in the non-Jewish hospital, I felt *Hakadosh Baruch Hu's* pain, as it were, and imagined Him calling out, "Where are My children?" When will the world realize that Hashem is the only Ruler of the world?

My musings were interrupted as I was paged to pray with a patient's family. Two parents stood in a room in the day surgery unit, awaiting their ten-year-old's open-heart surgery. And they wanted prayer.

Dad extended his hand for me to shake.

"I'm so sorry," I explained, putting on a warm smile. "I'm a religious Jew, and I'm not allowed to shake hands with a man unless he's my immediate family."

Mom looked like I had slapped her. "Can you run that by me again?" she asked.

I did.

"You can't even hold my husband's hand for prayer?" She was just not getting it.

"How 'bout if you and I hold hands, and your husband holds *your* hand?" I suggested to her. Thankfully, she accepted that idea.

And so I *davened*, asking Hashem to heal the little boy and let him enjoy longevity in good health. I asked Hashem to give strength to the boy and his parents, both during and after the surgery, and to give wisdom to the doctors and guide their hands to effect healing…

Mom hugged me and asked me to check in on them after the surgery was over. I wished them all well and made a special attempt to talk to Dad and soothe any bruised feelings.

I felt a little queasy after I left them, but, at the same time, encouraged. Had the two of them been truly offended by my religious principles, they wouldn't have asked me to come back, would they?

$$\dashv\!\wedge\!\text{\lower2pt\hbox{$\mathrm{\textstyle\mathsf{M}}$}}\!\wedge\!\text{\Large$\heartsuit$}$$

A YOUNG HEROINE

THE BEGINNING OF another endless twenty-four-hour shift. I'd just arrived at the hospital, and already I missed my family. *Just five more months to go of this program*, I tried consoling myself. *Yes, it's an eternity, but at least the finish line is in sight, right?*

But wait! Then I have to go out and actually get a chaplaincy job,

I realized. *It's not like there's retirement after these five months…* Sigh.

My day began with meeting a mother whose cancer-stricken son would be having a bone marrow transplant on Tuesday. The son was seventeen, while the woman's daughter, whose bone marrow was a perfect match and who was therefore going to be the donor, was only seven.

"We have to keep upbeat," the mother told me as she wiped her streaming eyes with tissues. "I have faith. I hope everything will be okay. And I certainly can't cry around Jay. He just looks at this as a little pause in his journey. 'After this,' he assures me, 'I'm going back to football practice.'"

"I haven't told my daughter that her marrow has the chance of saving Jay's life," the mother continued. "I don't want her to ever think, if, G-d forbid, something doesn't go well, that she did something wrong. I don't want her to carry that guilt."

Interesting, I mused. *I would have thought the right thing would be to make a big deal about what the little girl is doing, and tell her what a heroine she is for saving her brother's life!*

I wondered what she *did* tell her daughter; she couldn't exactly bring her to the hospital for surgery without telling her *anything!* But the mother wasn't forthcoming about any other information, so I resisted my urge to ask.

That day, I had to deliver a short, inspirational message in the chapel, and this mother was my only attendee there. (When I was on call to speak in the chapel, I always had to do so, even if no one showed up, because patients and families could tune in to my presentation through their TV channels in their rooms. So I never knew who was watching me, which, as an aside, was a great reminder to me about how Hashem always has His "camera" on us…) I chose to speak about Yosef, since we had just *leined Parshas Vayeishev.*

"Imagine Yosef: one minute, a favored, coddled son; the next minute, a degraded slave and then a prisoner, incarcerated because of a false accusation. Yet Yosef's attitude was calm and trusting in G-d. 'Why do you look so sad?' he asked the butler and baker, which gives us a powerful glimpse into who Yosef was. No matter what situation he found himself in, he wasn't sad; he remained upbeat, as he knew that G-d was guiding him on his life's path, and ultimately, it was all for his good, even if he didn't understand the reasons.

"Sometimes we may find ourselves thrown into a dark pit, like Yosef was, but we can still touch G-d's light if we remember Yosef's powerful message of acceptance, trust, and joy in the manifestation of G-d's plan."

I ended my presentation by *davening* for the health of the two children of the mother in the room with me, both the son who needed the transplant and the little sister who was giving of her own bone marrow to save her brother's life.

What an unbelievable challenge for a mother to go through, I marveled, shaking her hand. I wished her lots of strength and only good health for herself and her family.

As I walked away, my thoughts turned once again to my children back at home. Yes, I missed them, and I knew they missed me, too—but right now, all I could focus on was the appreciation I felt for the health of them all.

〜〜〜♡

MIRACLE IN OUR DAYS

SAD AND LONELY, I settled into the chaplaincy sleep room once again (why they call it that, I'll never know; for me, "sleep room" was an oxymoron). I was really feeling the downside of my whole program just then. It was the second night of Chanukah. My husband and children were at home lighting the menorah, filling the house with light and song, while I was away from them and all the festivities, holed up in a non-Jewish hospital, waiting for a pager to ring, though hoping it wouldn't…

And then, of course, it did precisely what I hoped it wouldn't do. Begone, feelings of despair! Forward march…

In a trauma room, an adorable eleven-month-old baby lay on the table struggling to breathe. Diagnosed with RSV (respiratory syncytial virus), he had taken a sudden downward turn. Both parents lovingly surrounded the little boy, but they could not get him quiet, and they couldn't hold him because of all of the tubes threading in and out of his body.

He looked so uncomfortable. My heart contracted, and I began to gently rub his stomach. Wonder of wonders! He calmed down. Yay!

The nurse explained that she had to stick a tube through his nose to do a quick procedure. In front of our eyes, just as she inserted the tube into the baby's nose, he suddenly stopped breathing! As the nurse yelled for back-up, panic registered in the parents' eyes. I stood next to them, silently hoping and *davening*. Tears coursed down their faces as they watched the team work on their baby. *Baruch Hashem*, the baby soon began to breathe again, and at that point, so did everyone else in the room. How fast life can change, from one moment to the next.

I left only when things had calmed down somewhat, and the baby—having been sedated—was resting comfortably. Things seemed more stable now, but boy, what a scare that had been!

Walking back to my office, I marveled at the miracle that had occurred before our eyes. And although the menorah's flames seemed far away, the power of Chanukah, of rejuvenation and miraculous intervention, felt very close.

$$\sim\!\!\!/\!\!\!\sim\!\!\!/\!\!\!\sim\!\!\!\heartsuit$$

ATTEMPTED SUICIDE

Two suicide attempts, one a week after the other. Both kids. *Ribono Shel Olam*! How? Why? What could be so bad in children's lives that would drive them to do such a thing?!

Scene 1:

I entered the room, noting a ten-year-old boy lying very still, hooked up to a ventilator, and a weepy mother on the phone. I walked toward Mom. She ended her call when I sat down next to her on the little couch near the window.

Mom: "I just don't know why Stevie would do such a thing."

Chaplain: "I'm so sorry, so very, very sorry."

Mom: "I wasn't feeling well. So I asked him to do the dishes. He got real angry and said he wouldn't do it; he hates doing the dishes. So I sent him to his room for some time-out."

Chaplain: (listening intently and nodding) "Uh-huh."

Mom: "Well, a little while later, I sent my five-year-old, Mike, to tell him he could come out. Mike came running out to tell me that he found Stevie hanging with a belt around his neck. 'I took it off,' Mike said, showing me the belt. 'Now Stevie is sleeping.'

"I jumped up to see what was going on, and quickly called 911. It took them half an hour to get to us; we live out in the sticks. And now…here we are…"

I waited with Mom through the CT scan, mostly listening as she poured out her heart to me. I found out that they had no money, that her ex-husband did not follow through on his child support obligations, and that she was currently unemployed. A recipe for disaster, all right, but to this extent?

I prayed with Mom for Stevie's recovery, saddened that this young boy might have succeeded in taking his own life. So tragic… Several days later, I found out the results of all the testing: Due to what Steve had done to himself, he was now permanently, severely brain damaged.

Poor boy. Poor family.

Scene 2:

"You might want to go into Room 18," a nurse advised me. "A teenage girl was just admitted." Lowering her voice, she added, "Ingestion. I just thought you might want to know."

What does that mean? I wondered.

"Meaning…?" I ventured, feeling foolish for asking.

"She tried to kill herself," the nurse replied, sounding angry and upset. "And that medicine that she took is a whole lot stronger than Tylenol. I just don't know what's gonna be…"

I gulped. Yuck! Another one?!

This girl looked older than the other child. She was sixteen; he was only ten. She, too, lay in bed, breathing with the help of a ventilator. Both parents were there.

"I'm so sorry," I murmured, putting my hand on Mom's shoulder and feeling an awful sense of déjà vu. She, too, was sitting on that same kind of couch in the back of a room in the Pediatric ICU.

She turned to me with tears running down her cheeks. "I just know she's gonna be okay. It's just getting through this."

I nodded, wondering how she knew that her daughter would be okay. Had the staff told her that her daughter would recover?

We prayed for her daughter's full health and recovery. She thanked me for coming in; I thanked Hashem for letting me get out of there…

May all of us, and all of our children, always embrace the tremendous gift of life that we have!

⊰~~~♡

FRIENDLY ENCOUNTER WITH THE POLICE

When doing my clinical hours, I used to be able to park in the hospital parking lot. But a few months into doing my training at the children's hospital, the hospital became stricter about this and no longer allowed us chaplains-in-training to park on campus, due to space shortages. They even threatened to give us tickets if we used their lot.

This meant that I now had to park my car about a mile from the hospital. I resented the distance I had to walk. The extra exercise wasn't a bad thing; it was more the time factor and the principle of the matter that irritated me. After all, we were working for the hospital pro bono! You would think the least they could do was allow us to park in their lot.

One morning, I arrived at my new, usual parking place, outside a public park a few blocks from the hospital, and, to my chagrin, I found the gate to the lot locked. I checked the sign above the gate: yup, it should have been open already. It was 8:05 a.m., and the sign said the parking lot opened at 8:00 a.m.

Ho-hum. What do I do now? I thought to myself.

Suddenly, a police car pulled up alongside me. Immediately, my heart began doing a fluttery dance. What did the police want from me? Was it illegal for me to park in this lot?

The policeman didn't move from his place. *Well, may as well get this unpleasantness over with*, I decided. I stepped out of my car and approached the passenger side of his vehicle.

"You're not mad at me, are ya?" the officer, a tall man with whitening hair and a broad smile, asked me. Apparently it was his job to open the gate at 8:00 a.m., and he was late today.

Surprised, I grinned and returned his line with one of my own: "I'll forgive you this time!"

I was amused by the irony of this conversation. To think that a civilian would entertain the thought of showing anger to a police officer!

"Y'know," the officer said, "I saw you the other day"—*oh, boy, he's been watching me!*—"and I thought, *Isn't that smart! She works over at the hospital and parks here. Then she doesn't have to pay for parking!"*

Whoa. I'm overwhelmed. Not only is he not angry with me, but this policeman just gave me a compliment!

"I'm a chaplain intern," I told him. "I work at the children's hospital."

"Really now?" His smile grew broader. "I'm taking a chaplaincy course, too, over at my seminary. I may just want to work at your place when I'm done."

"I can give you contact information if that would be helpful," I offered. "We'd love to have you on board."

"Well, thanks. But sometimes I wonder if I'm too old to be a chaplain."

"I don't think so," I said, wondering how many of my wrinkles were visible. "In my opinion, maturity and life experience are assets for a chaplain."

"Maybe. I wish I could give you a ride over there, but regulations don't allow."

That's okay. I don't know that I would want to ride in a police car, thank you very much.

"I appreciate the thought," I said, slinging my pocketbook over my shoulder. "And good luck to you with everything."

He smiled. "You have yourself a great day."

"You, too," I replied.

How nice to find a person—and a friendly one, at that—beneath the steely policeman uniform. Imagine that!

⎯∿∿∿∿♡⎯

HEAD-ON COLLISION

THE PAGER SANG its summons, and I called back the number that came up on the screen. "This is Chaplain Rachel, returning your page."

"Yes, Chaplain. One of our cleaning staff members got some bad news here; her mother was just killed in a car accident. Would you come down to her, please?"

What can I possibly do to help? I wondered to myself. Nevertheless, I strode down the long hallway, my pace quickening as I thought about what was going on. What would I find when I got to this woman? How hysterical would she be?

A nurse led me to a consult room in the emergency department. Immediately, my eyes took in a dark-haired woman in a cleaning staff uniform, red-eyed and sniffling. I sat down beside her on the couch and put my hand on her shoulder.

"I'm so sorry," I murmured.

Her cell phone rang.

"Oh, Dr. Moss," she cried into the phone, "it was a head-on collision. My mother was picking up my daughter from school, and an eighteen-year-old driver barreled into them. And now… they just told me she's gone…"

The woman's weeping intensified, and I held her hand while continuing to massage her shoulder. When she put down the phone, I asked her if she wanted a hug. She clung to me like she never wanted to let go.

"This is so hard," she finally said, releasing her grip and looking into my eyes. "It's gonna be a process, isn't it?"

"Yes, it is a process," I replied softly. "Give yourself as much time as you need. Whatever you feel is normal. Please make sure you have support, people around to talk to."

"Yes," she said with a shuddering breath. "My daughter is in one of these rooms here, alone; I should probably go and be with her. I'm a single mom, you know, and I have to work long hours... Jamie stayed over at my mother's all the time while I was away at work... I know she senses that something bad happened...but how do I tell her that her beloved grandma's gone?"

"Would it make it easier if I come with you?" I offered.

"Yes," she said.

We walked down the hall together and into her daughter's examination room. Jamie looked to be about nine or ten. She had come away from the crash with a fractured pelvis, and she lay in the hospital bed with tears in her eyes.

"How're you feeling, Baby?" Her mother smoothed her hair back.

"It hurts," she replied.

"Honey, I have bad news." Mom took a deep breath. "We lost Grandma."

"What?" Jamie's eyes opened wide, disbelievingly. "Grandma's—dead? But how...? What...? Who's gonna do my laundry, cook my meals?"

We all smiled a little, and her mother reassured her. "I will."

Wow, what a grandma, I marveled. Everyone could use a grandma like that.

"Will I be able to live with you now?" Jamie asked her mother.

Looking a little startled, Mom quickly said, "Yes, yes, of course."

Mom held her for a little while, and then went out to make a call.

"I'm so sorry," I told Jamie.

"This is the worst day ever," she said. She paused and then said, "You know the last words I heard Grandma say after the crash? They were, 'Where's my grandchild?'"

"That means she said, 'I love you,'" I told Jamie, holding her hand. "She gave you a gift. It sounds like the two of you were very close."

"She raised me," the girl cried. "I don't know how I'll go on without her!"

"I'm sorry," I said again.

Her tears continued to flow, and I did my best to comfort her.

After about an hour of conversation with both Jamie and her mother, I felt that they were composed enough for me to leave.

"I wish you G-d's comfort and strength," I told the mother as we hugged each other. "Give yourself lots of time and support. I'm here Wednesdays and Thursdays, and there's always a chaplain around here if you just want to talk. Please take care of yourself."

Then I turned to Jamie. "Feel better, sweetie, in every way. Remember how much your grandmother loved you and still does. That will never go away." I bent down to kiss her forehead before giving a final wave and leaving.

A beloved mother and grandmother, gone in an instant. How quickly the tide of life can change. As many times as I see it, I doubt I will ever get used to it.

SEIZING THE MOMENT

"A PATIENT'S MOM could use someone to talk to," the nurse

told me when I answered her page, late one night while I was on call. "Would you come up to speak to her?"

It's already midnight! Can't it wait until morning? I thought, trying to rouse myself from my exhausted state.

Come on, there are only four "on call" days left of this program for you, Rachel, I tried to encourage myself. *You'll get through this.*

"Sure, of course," I replied, hoping my voice sounded calm and professional. "I'll be up soon."

The room was dark when I knocked and entered. A black mother sat close to her son's hospital bed, her eyes brimming with tears. My heart contracted in pity to see someone in such obvious pain.

"This is really rough for you," I commented.

She nodded. "My grandma just died last week; my husband is in prison and probably will never get out; and now this. I'm just so scared."

I found myself insanely curious about what her husband had done to earn himself life imprisonment, and hoped she would tell me in the course of our conversation.

"Of course you're scared. Each one of those situations is huge, and you've got them all together!"

"I just want to be there for Xavier," she pointed to her son lying in bed, sleeping, "but I don't know what to do. I haven't eaten or slept…they don't know what's wrong with him…what can I do…?"

"You're doing the best thing for your son that any mother can do—you're here with him at his side."

She nodded. "It's just so hard…"

"Of course it is," I sympathized. "Do you have support, some family or friends?"

"No, I'm really alone. Just taking care of my kids… I don't

really have any close friends."

I was pretty struck by that one. How does one survive without friends?

"Do you believe in G-d?" I ventured, taking a chance.

She nodded again.

"Would you like me to say a prayer?"

"Okay."

I said my usual "prayer for the patient," asking Hashem to heal the child; to give the medical personnel the wisdom they needed to help cure him. I also asked for strength for the mother, so that she could get through these huge hurdles that seemed to keep sweeping toward her like massive waves, knocking her down with their force.

And then suddenly, Xavier, her big, strapping, fifteen-year-old son, began to have a seizure! His entire body started shaking violently; his limbs flailed and thrashed.

Xavier's mother screamed loud and long.

I jumped; I hadn't been expecting the high-pitched, strident scream! Realizing how unprofessional that was, I quickly pulled myself together and put my arm around the mother's shoulder, holding her close while two nurses ran in to tend to her son.

"Xavier, are you okay?" one nurse asked him. She peered into his face, trying to get a response, but nothing was forthcoming.

"Xavier, you just had another seizure. Are you okay?"

To me, that sounded almost as intelligent as asking someone who just smashed his head on a hard surface, "Are you okay?" In my opinion, Xavier certainly was *not* okay. Not that anyone was asking me, of course.

Xavier's mother and I watched him, my arm still protectively encircling her, and I found myself holding my breath as we waited for Xavier to respond. Had the seizure affected his brain?

Finally, about five minutes later, he opened his eyes and responded slightly to the nurse's questions. Then he rolled over and went back to sleep.

"We want you to be okay, too," one of the nurses said as she approached Xavier's mother. "If you get sick, then we'll have to send you to the hospital across the street, and you won't be able to be with Xavier. So have something to eat, and then I'll find you a place to lie down. I promise we'll call you if we need you, no matter what time it is."

Mom agreed to this plan, and the nurse assured her that she would get her a sandwich from the cafeteria.

"I can only imagine how scary it is to see your son doing that," the nurse continued, and I silently applauded her for her empathy. "I have two kids of my own, and I have a hard time watching anything bad happening to them." She patted Mom's shoulder and then left.

"I wonder if you can close your eyes," I suggested, loosening my grip on Mom a little.

Once again, she nodded, never taking her eyes off of her son. Eventually, her eyes closed.

"I'm going to go," I said softly, and this time *she* jumped.

"I'm sorry," I soothed, wishing I hadn't disturbed her. "I didn't mean to startle you. You rest, and the nurse will be here soon with your food. I hope your son recovers quickly, and if you need me again, please tell them to page me."

Nodding, she closed her eyes again, and I left. And suddenly, I recalled the time when one of my own children had had a seizure. It had been on a Friday night. My daughter had been eighteen months old at the time, and she'd spiked a very sudden, high fever—and soon after, she'd had the seizure. We immediately called an ambulance and ran her to the hospital. But I remember that fear, the sheer terror of holding my baby and watching her body shake and flail uncontrollably, and then her eyes roll back, until she fainted.

"Breathe, breathe!" I'd begged her through my tears.

"That's my baby," I'd whimpered to the EMT sitting next to me in the ambulance. "Will she be okay?"

Baruch Hashem, my daughter's seizure turned out to be "just" a febrile one, caused by the high fever that had raged in her body. But it had been a searing experience for us all nonetheless.

My thoughts traveled back to Xavier and his mother, and I hoped that their story, too, would have a happy ending.

⎍⎍⎍♡

LENDING SUPPORT IN A STICKY SITUATION

ONCE, I WAS paged to the emergency department to support a mother whose child had been in an accident and was being taken in for surgery.

"I'm sorry," I murmured, and she clasped my hand.

"Will you pray with me?" she wanted to know.

"Sure," I replied.

And then, before I knew what hit me, the mother sank to her knees, closed her eyes, and began invoking you-know-whose name! And not just once, but over and over again!

I felt tremors going up and down my spine. There was no way I could pray with this obviously devout Christian woman—this was way out of my league, and I wanted to bolt from the room. Yet as she kneeled and prayed, pouring her heart out and shedding copious tears, I knew that running away wasn't an option; I had to stay beside this woman.

Determinedly focusing my thoughts on Hashem, the only

One there is to turn to, I placed my hands on the woman's shoulders, conveying my support to her while tuning out the rest of what she was doing…

⸎

MY LIFELINE, MY LOYAL COMPANIONS

FINALLY, IN THE last few weeks of my chaplaincy program, I had a Jewish family to visit in the hospital! While of course I wasn't happy that a Jewish child had to be in the hospital, I can't describe my excitement at seeing *frum* faces while at work.

Not only that, but I even knew the family from our community! My daughter was friends with one of their daughters, and we actually had that girl stay over at our house while her parents were in the hospital with her sick sister, Raizy.

While doing my clinical hours, I stopped in to visit Raizy and her parents and see how they were doing. As we talked, we discussed the hardships of awaiting a diagnosis, having a child in pain, and the added stress of taking off from work.

"It's all my fault," Raizy said, looking sad.

"Why do you think so?" I asked her.

"Well…" She grinned, blushing. "Maybe it's not *all* my fault…"

Suddenly, Raizy glanced at her watch and let out a yelp. "It's almost *chatzos!*" she cried. "Ma, I forgot my siddur, and I didn't *daven* yet!"

"I have a siddur," I offered, my heart leaping with joy. What a privilege to actually be able to give someone a siddur! I ran down to the chaplaincy office and got her my siddur and Tehillim. Those two were my lifelines in this Christian environment, witnesses to my supreme loneliness and my heart's outpouring over the last two years. This was the same siddur that had prodded me to stay in the chaplaincy program and not give up, during that initial and oh, so difficult orientation a lifetime ago (had only two years passed since then?).

As I handed over these two precious *sefarim* to Raizy, I felt like I was giving away cherished friends. When I *davened* in the chaplaincy office over the next few days, I missed my brown leather companions, but I comforted myself with the knowledge that they were doing a vital task.

Baruch Hashem, Raizy went home soon after, and my siddur and Tehillim were returned to my office to await my next *tefillos*. Although I'd been thrilled to lend the two out, I was equally thrilled to have them back. They were my anchors in this foreign world, my trusted and loyal friends and confidantes.

⎯〰⎯♡

WHEN I TOLD my supervisor about my first hospital encounter with religious Jews in my two-year-plus stint, and how I'd been able to help them out by lending my prayer books, she smiled.

"I'll bet you'll want to take those prayer books home with you when you're done here," she said.

"No," I said quickly, "I want the prayer books to be here for others who may need them at some time. That's why our Bikur Cholim organization brought them to the hospital in the first place."

But when I came back to the hospital for my next night shift, I was surprised by my strong desire to yes, take "my" siddur and Tehillim home with me. My supervisor was right, I realized. The siddur and Tehillim had taken this journey with me, and indeed, it *would* be hard to leave them when I finished my unit. It would almost be like leaving a part of my heart behind.

My dear siddur, I thought, gazing fondly at its brown leather cover. *May you bring solace to another Yid whose heart craves connection. May you help his or her* tefillos *ascend straight to the* Kisei Hakavod. *And may there come a time when we won't need to cry out in pain anymore; a time when our tears of sorrow will come to an end,* b'meheirah b'yameinu.

BETWEEN A ROCK AND A HARD PLACE

WHILE STILL IN the midst of my training, a sixty-year-old woman in our community turned to Bikur Cholim for assistance. Her father's health was declining due to his Alzheimer's. She tried valiantly to keep him living in her home, where she had built a special suite for him, but she was finding the burden of his care increasingly difficult. Once again, due to a fall, he was hospitalized and then admitted into a nursing home for rehabilitation.

Bertha needed support during her upcoming meeting with the nursing home staff. So the night after my overnight in the hospital, off I went to help her out with this.

When the meeting began, I introduced myself as Bertha's friend and a hospital chaplain. A number of eyebrows lifted when I used the title. I only said it because I figured it would help Bertha's cause. But after years of naming "housewife" as my occupation, it did stoke my ego to see that these professionals were impressed by my new title. Being a wife and mother will always be my highest priority in my life—but I'll admit it: those raised eyebrows were fun to watch!

I stayed with Bertha throughout the meeting while her father's care and progress were evaluated. Now that she was finally coming to terms with the fact that she couldn't continue providing care for him at home, she was running into the brick walls of insurance regulations. Unfortunately, her father did not have long-term care insurance. And that was causing major problems.

Bertha told the staff that she was applying for Medicaid long-term care insurance. Then she asked the following question:

"If we're accepted, and my father becomes a resident in your nursing home, what benefits will he receive? Will he continue getting all of the therapies that he is getting now? As I've been told, even though his decline is inevitable, with regard to whatever he *is* still capable of, if you don't use it, you lose it. So anything we can do to maintain his agility will be beneficial."

Gently but firmly, the staff explained to her that once her father had met his therapeutic goals, he probably would not receive any more therapy.

"But," Bertha said, her eyes glistening, "then he'll just keep declining."

"Therapy is designed to bring a patient only so far," a nurse explained. "Once he is at that point, he is taken off the regimen. Unless, of course, something happens; then he is reassessed and put back on again, according to his needs. It's unfortunate, but because Alzheimer's is a chronic condition, the therapies for it don't continue forever. We can only help him recover from his recent fall."

"So maybe I *should* bring him home," Bertha cried out. "I can't just let him go down!"

"I'm sorry," the nurse said gently, patting Bertha's shoulder. "I'm really sorry."

Bertha took a minute to gather her composure, and then we toured the long-term care section of the facility.

One resident that we passed by was emitting animal-like shrieks and screams.

"My father will go nuts if I keep him here," Bertha murmured. "I sure hope he won't have this woman as a neighbor."

And then, after a moment's pause, she added, "How can I do this to him? I wouldn't want someone to do this to me, to put me away. I'm killing him!"

"No, Bertha." I gave her a hug. "You're doing the best you can. You can't take care of him anymore. And if you get sick, then who's going to be there for him?"

Why does getting old have to be so hard? I looked deeply into Bertha's eyes, and her twin pools of pained understanding gazed back at me.

Back at home later that day, I said to my husband, "Let's not get old."

Then, thinking better of that comment, I quickly amended it. "Wait, *chas v'shalom*. Let's get old, but stay healthy. How's that?"

IT JUST AIN'T FAIR!

I was called by a nurse in the CICU (Cardiac Intensive Care Unit) to support a family whose child had just received a very sobering diagnosis.

"I'm so sorry," I began, looking first at the mother, cradling her five-week-old, and then at the father, sitting at her side. "I heard you got some bad news."

Mom was crying softly, and I put my hand on her shoulder.

"I'm in a state of shock," Dad said.

"You had no idea," I said. "Healthy pregnancy, healthy baby, or so it seemed…" That's what I'd been told.

Dad shook his head and looked from me to the baby. "It just ain't fair," he said.

"Do you want to share what the doctor told you?" I asked him gently.

"The doctor said that…that Dayton has a 50 percent chance of living till he's five," he gulped.

What could I say? Mom continued weeping, and I continued to massage her shoulder.

"The left side of his heart never developed," Mom whispered.

"What can I do to help you?" I asked. All I wanted was to wave a magic wand and take away the couple's searing pain.

"Pray," Dad said.

"Almighty G-d," I began, "please grant wisdom to the doctors and nurses to heal Baby Dayton. We know that the medical team is Your earthly agent, but the ultimate decisions are in Your hands. May Dayton grow healthy and strong and live to bring joy to his wonderful family, community, and all who know him. Please, G-d, watch over little Dayton throughout his illness, and give his parents strength during this trying time. Amen."

I stayed with the parents for quite a while. When Dad began to cry, my heart melted. Something about a man's tears always breaks my heart. Is it because I grew up without a father?

"It don't make sense," Dayton's father kept chanting, broken-record-style. "It don't make sense."

"Is there anything from your faith that can give you strength to get through this?" I asked. Ever so grateful for my anchor of *Yiddishkeit*, I tapped into my certainty that everything Hashem does has a careful plan and reason; that even though we don't understand Hashem's ways, we know that everything He does is ultimately for our good… I've heard this sentiment echoed by many of the "believing" families here, and I was hoping that Baby Dayton's parents would be able to internalize this truth, too.

"I want a miracle," the father answered, and I nodded slowly. Well, that was a little out of my jurisdiction, but how I wished…

"I'll be praying for you," I told the parents, preparing to take my leave. "I hope you get your miracle. All the best, and if you need me at any time tonight, feel free to have the nurses page me; they know how to reach me. Take care."

A seemingly healthy baby—a fourth child…no inkling beforehand that anything was amiss…and now there were two young parents sitting with their critically ill infant, who was fighting for his life.

THE IMPOSSIBLE DREAM

A LIGHT SHONE from the end of the tunnel; it was almost time to say goodbye to my chaplaincy office where I had spent so much time over the last two years. It was around then that I went out with my friend Shifra for coffee.

Shifra is a chaplain, too, only she graduated her training program a while ago and is already working as a regular chaplain for some time now, in a Jewish hospice.

Shifra and I typically enjoy a yearly get-together. As we leave our annual meeting with a hug and a wave, we always say, "Let's not wait a year until next time!" But as busy wives, mothers, and community activists, our socialization time is limited, and it usually ends up taking another year until we get together again.

Now, as we sat and talked, she asked me to describe one of my most memorable experiences of my chaplaincy training. "Only if you want to," she added.

"Memorable Jewish-wise, emotionally, or both?" I asked.

She shrugged, so I said, "I'll give you both."

I described two poignant episodes that remained with me, and then reflected the question back to her.

Shifra thought for a moment. Then she said, "Let me show you."

She pulled out her cell phone and proceeded to show me a video that, even now, continues to play in my mind and heart. It is one of the most powerful things I have ever seen...

Shifra walks into Ellen's room and pulls up a chair next to her bed. Ellen is an old lady on hospice care who has not spoken a word in four years. She has end-stage Alzheimer's, and has not touched a morsel of food in several days. The end seems imminent. Her skin looks dry and withered, and her eyes don't focus on her visitor; she is in her own world.

Knowing that Ellen used to sing beautifully and has always had a love for music, Shifra decides to sing with her. From a previous encounter with the family, Shifra knows that Ellen's all-time favorite song is "The Impossible Dream."

So Shifra, a talented vocalist in her own right, begins to sing "The Impossible Dream."

Her voice rings out like an angel's, touching notes that surely reach the Heavens. And I watch, mesmerized by the magic that unfolds as...Ellen begins to sing along! The voice that had not spoken in four years is actually singing! And the eyes that have been clouded for four years become clear.

Before my eyes, Ellen's lips shape the words of her favorite song, and her voice joins Shifra's. Shifra strokes Ellen's arm, and Ellen looks into her eyes and continues to lift her voice. Ellen's notes are discordant, but her song is the most glorious melody that I have ever been privileged to hear.

It is a song of life, a song of hope, a song of triumph. It is a song of the soul.

When Shifra sings the part about being laid to rest, Ellen's eyes flicker, and tears spring to my own eyes…

As I watched the video over and over again later that afternoon (I had Shifra email it to me), I was transported to a different place and time. You see, "The Impossible Dream" was one of my mother's favorite songs, too. In those magical moments while I sat with Shifra and Ellen, watching the unbelievable clip, my mother joined me. My mother, who died one month short of her forty-eighth birthday, also had a golden voice. She would sing when she vacuumed and thought no one was listening. But I heard, and her voice carved a niche in my *neshamah*.

Watching Shifra and Ellen sing together, it dawned on me that I really was witnessing "The Impossible Dream." For as death hovered in the air, life was sparked through a touch of caring, song, and love. Ellen surrendered her soul four hours later, Shifra told me. But her song lives on.

That's why I want to be a chaplain, I realized. I want the opportunity to make a difference in people's lives in this way.

CHAPLAINCY ACCREDITATION: WHAT DOES IT INVOLVE?

Does the field of chaplaincy spark your interest? If your answer is a resounding yes, this is what's involved in becoming a chaplain:

For starters, you need to have some kind of background in theology in order to be accepted into a chaplaincy program. If you attended seminary or learned in yeshivah, and therefore hold the equivalence of a Master's in divinity, you're good to go.

To obtain a regular job as a chaplain in any facility, four credits are optimal (though in Atlanta, where I live, the field is very competitive, so many chaplains opt for five credits. I had many prospective employers turn me down because I "only" had four credits.).

To get your four credits, you can take four extended units, consisting of four hundred hours per unit. There is no pay offered for these courses; in fact, you will probably have to pay for the education. That was the route I took. The other option is, after completing your first extended unit, to take a full-time residency. This does offer a stipend. But what full-time residency means is basically giving up your life for a full year; it is a forty-hour work week, in addition to assignments and being on call several times a month. But at least you know that when that year is over, you're done. So if you can handle it, go for it!

Once you are a certified Jewish chaplain, you should be able to work predominantly with Jewish patients in the facility where you find employment, though you may be asked to see non-Jews as well.

May Hashem bless all of your endeavors with resounding success! And may we all merit to make a *kiddush Hashem* wherever we go and whatever we do.

PART 6
STEPPING BACK INTO NORMAL LIFE

ONCE MY PROGRAM was over, I spent some time looking for a job and some time feeling bored and out-of-sorts. I had been so busy and overwhelmed before, and now I awoke each morning without knowing exactly where I would go each day and what I would accomplish. I filled out endless online applications for chaplaincy jobs and made numerous phone calls, yet a job didn't materialize.

But Bikur Cholim continued…

A REMARKABLE RESURGENCE

"RACHEL, CALL ME back…"

I picked up my cell phone message and immediately knew

from Malka's voice that there was bad news. She sounded choked up, and I knew her daughter had just gone into hospice yesterday; it didn't take much to put the pieces together.

"Malka?" I whispered, my heart in my throat.

"Becky died," she said, telling me what I had already surmised.

"*Baruch Dayan Ha'emes*," I whispered. "Oh, Malka, I'm so sorry."

"I was there today," she told me, crying. "I just got home when they called me and told me she took a turn for the worse. Before I knew if I could get back, she was gone."

The image of Malka sitting in her living room with only her Persian cat for company was like the picture of a tree in midwinter, its skeletal branches a shadow of their former selves, gray and cold and alone. Malka's daughter had lived with her; now she would be alone. Her two other children had unfortunately intermarried and distanced themselves from their parents. Her husband, Sam, had passed on years before, and Malka had no other family in town.

I'm going over there, I decided.

I went to Malka's house and sat with her while she massaged her fluffy, oversized, cream-colored cat. Our conversation kept getting interrupted by phone calls, while loud purring provided background music.

"Excuse me," Malka apologized. "It's the funeral director."

I listened as she gave him names, spellings, and birth dates of all her extended family. He wanted English and Hebrew names, where each person was born, where they all lived, and more. *Really*, I was thinking, starting to feel exasperated. *Why does he have to take care of the paperwork at a time like this? The woman's closest relative just died! Can't he let her be?*

And just when I found myself struggling mightily, wishing I

could pull the phone away from her because enough was enough, Malka put the man in his place.

"Would you like my cat's name and date of birth, too?" she asked. "Becky was very close to our cat, you know."

Leave it to Malka, I thought. Even at a time like this, she didn't lose her sense of humor; she had an indomitable strength that, I hoped, would get her through this tremendously difficult time.

But even strong people have their limits. Malka was battling her own illness, and within days after *shivah* for her daughter ended, she wound up in the hospital.

This time a nurse from the hospital called me. It was Erev Shabbos, and I was knee-deep in cooking.

"It's serious," the nurse said. "They're not sure if she's going to make it."

"I can be there in a little over an hour," I told her. "Let me just throw some food together so she'll have what to eat."

"Forget the food," the nurse said. "Please. Just come now."

"Forget the food?" I repeated dumbly, my Jewish-mother instincts rebelling at the thought.

"She can't eat anything right now, anyway," the nurse said. "I think it's important that you just come as soon as you can."

So come I did. By the time I got to the hospital, the scare had thankfully passed.

"She's doing better," the nurse assured me when I came into the hospital room. "I simply told her that it wasn't her time yet."

I let out the breath I had been holding.

"Malka?" I approached her bed and grasped her hand. Her face was covered by an oxygen mask.

"Can you believe this?" she wheezed. "This is too much."

I had to agree. To lose her daughter and then wind up in the

ICU did seem over the top.

As I continued to visit her over the new few weeks of her recuperation, both in the hospital and back at home, Malka unloaded her story to me. And what a story it was.

Malka was the proprietor of a Jewish bookstore in the neighborhood. Unknown to her loyal patrons and friends, she was struggling valiantly to make ends meet. Both her and her daughter's illnesses had taken a major toll on their finances, and they were months behind on the store's rent.

Shortly before Becky's final illness, Malka's landlord threatened that if she didn't pay in full by that Friday, she would be evicted. Well, Malka could not come up with the money by then, and a few days later Becky passed away, but the landlord was true to his word, Malka's personal circumstances notwithstanding. To add insult to injury, the landlord also laid claim to all of Malka's valuables in lieu of the money he didn't expect to see. He confiscated silver menorahs, candlesticks, and other assorted, expensive Judaica items, estimating their worth to be equivalent to Malka's debts.

"So you see," Malka sighed, "I've lost two thirds of my life. I've lost my daughter, my health, and my business. In one fell swoop." And she began to cry.

I had no words. The poor woman. Her ship was adrift in a stormy sea, with seemingly no lighthouse in sight to guide her. But while I mulled over her sorry set of circumstances, I forgot I was dealing with an indomitable spirit named Malka.

As the weeks passed, Malka struggled to regain her strength. Always she'd assure me, with a twinkle in her eyes, that her time had not yet come, so she simply *had* to rebound. And one day, when I dropped by to visit, I was amazed to see a tray of her famous chocolate crescent horns cooling on the stovetop.

"Wow!" I said, thoroughly impressed as I admired their perfect forms and inhaled the intoxicating fragrance. "How'd you do this?"

"I was bored," she said with a shrug. That was when I knew Malka was going to be okay.

"Have some," she offered me. Then, as we sat at her kitchen table, over steaming cups of coffee and chocolate crescent horns, she said, "Let me ask you a question. Do you think I should try to get back into business?" Hope danced in her eyes, and a wisp of a smile played on her lips.

Was she serious? Was she delusional? With all of her health restrictions and her financial situation, I wasn't sure if it was at all realistic for Malka to think about starting up her business again. How in the world could she rebuild from ashes?

But hey, who says we Jews are realists? From our very inception, we've been birthed and sustained on miracles, ever since the ancient times of Avraham and Sarah, straight into our own era.

"You know," I answered, warming to the idea, "maybe you can start small. It's worth a try."

I kissed her weathered cheek and got up to go.

"I'll let you know what happens, Rachel," she assured me.

It's good to believe, I thought, getting into my car and driving home. *It's good to dream.*

And I resolved to fill out the job applications waiting for me at home.

THE WEB OF MITZVAH INTRIGUE

It was the shortest Erev Shabbos of the year when the call came in.

"Rachel, you know Esther Marks is in the hospital?" It was my Bikur Cholim partner, Michele.

"She is?" I gasped. "What's going on?"

"Her heart," Michele told me. "They need to put in a stent; her arteries are blocked."

"*Oy!*" I exclaimed, my own heart aflutter as I started to set my Shabbos table. "What does she need?"

"Her daughter said she would love some food. She's not really happy with the hospital frozen kosher dinners."

Esther was divorced, doing her best to hold up her splintered world on her own. And now she had to deal with this medical issue, on top of everything else. I felt terrible for her.

"Um," I murmured, folding napkins and trying to decide if I could handle this mitzvah right now. Would I have time to run to the hospital with the food? On the other hand, how could I not? Esther needed to eat, and I couldn't start making calls now to find someone else who could take the food to her.

Nor, I realized, did I want to. There was something about the challenge of this mitzvah that beckoned me.

"I'll go," I said aloud.

"Are you sure?" Michele asked. "Maybe I can do it instead?"

"No, I'll do it," I assured her, ignoring the voice inside me that insisted, *This is crazy. Don't do it.*

"How 'bout if I go with you?" Michele offered. "We could probably get it delivered a lot faster like that."

"That sounds great," I replied. We quickly divvied up who would bring what for Esther. "I can go by three."

"That's exactly when my cake will be ready." I could almost see Michele smiling into the phone. "I'll pick you up then."

At 3:00 p.m. sharp, Michele beeped, and I zoomed into her minivan with my foil wrapped packages. We arrived at the hospital by 3:20; *licht bentching* was 5:15. We marathon-walked, panting our way to Esther's room, knocked, entered, and—surprise! The room was empty.

Michele and I looked at each other blankly, and, with unspoken accord, marched to the nurse's station.

"Hi there," I began, getting the attention of a nurse. Seeing her take in our snood-covered heads through narrowed eyes, I got the distinct feeling that she didn't want to be bothered by the likes of us. "We came to bring food for our friend, Esther Marks, and she's not in her room. Do you know where she is?"

"She just went home," the nurse replied indifferently. "You just missed her."

Michele and I locked gazes again, and I saw my expression of shock and confusion mirrored in her eyes.

"But I just spoke with her daughter a few hours ago!" Michele protested. "She was supposed to be here!"

The nurse just shrugged.

Just then, a doctor, whose name tag read the distinctly Jewish name "Michael Cohen," passed by. "Something smells good," he said to us with a smile. I looked at his yarmulke-less head and wondered where this would lead.

"Would you like some challah?" Michele offered in her charming South African accent, with a gracious smile of her own.

"I wish I could," he answered, "but with the risk of germs here, I really can't accept outside food. Thanks anyway." His eyes were warm, and my mind spun lofty dreams. Would this exchange bring a lost Jew back to the fold? Maybe Hashem had sent us on this wild goose chase for this doctor's sake?

"Maybe there's another Jewish patient who needs the food," Michele suggested, interrupting my reverie, and I marveled at the thought. Overwhelmed by disappointment that our mitzvah had backfired, I had assumed that we would simply turn around and go back home, with our hands as full as when we'd come.

"Not that I know of," the nurse said laconically.

"Let's call the chaplain's office," I said, feeling Michele's flicker of hope kindle in my heart.

"Chaplain Libby here," a chaplain answered, and I plunged into our story. Chaplain Libby turned on her computer and tried to access her census to see if she could find a Jewish patient.

"My computer's frozen," she said. "I'm sorry, but I can't get into the census."

Meanwhile, Michele was on her cell phone, trying to figure out why Esther had been suddenly discharged and if she needed any help.

"Esther still needs the food," Michele told me. "Her kids are invited out for the meals, but she'll be staying home."

My heart lifted; at least we would still be able to help Esther out with the food. But what of our hospital Shabbos box containing electric candlesticks, matzah, grape juice, a *bentcher*, a Jewish magazine, and a cute Bikur Cholim magnet with our contact information?

Michele and I power-walked toward the elevators; the time was 3:45 p.m. We passed an information desk that was minus an information-giving-occupant, and inspiration struck. Calling the chaplain's office once more, we described our "Sabbath box," asking Chaplain Libby if we could leave the box under the information desk, with her name on it. Maybe the hospital would have a Jewish patient at some point who would appreciate the box?

"Sure," she said. "That desk is on my way out. I'll pick up the box and hold onto it. Thank you for your thoughtfulness."

Michele and I dropped the box there and then ran to the parking lot, where we quickly found her van. But as we merged into the bumper-to-bumper, late-afternoon traffic, our hearts sank like leaden balls in a lake. I fervently wished that I could affix a propeller to the top of the van so we could just fly home.

"Let's try the highway," I said to Michele as we inched forward. In the meantime, both of us whipped out our cell phones and called our respective homes, tersely giving our husbands instructions about how to warm up our families' Shabbos food.

Please, Hashem, I begged silently, *let us get home in time. Shluchei mitzvah einan nizakin* (those who do mitzvos do not come to any harm)… After fifteen endless minutes of nearly standstill traffic, we merged onto the highway and began to breathe as our van zoomed forward.

"I still have a bunch of last-minute things to do around the house before Shabbos," Michele remarked, as our exit came into view. It was 4:15 p.m.

"Me, too." I grinned. "We'll be fine, *b'ezras Hashem.*"

"Do you want me to drop you off first?" she offered. "I can go myself to bring the food to Esther."

"No," I said, knowing that Esther's street came before mine. "We're in this together. I'm so glad you came with me, by the way."

"Oh, I'm so happy we're doing this together, too," she answered. "I would've been an absolute wreck if I were by myself."

"We'll be fine," I said again, trying to reassure both of us as we chugged up Esther's steep driveway. Throwing the van doors open, we ran out with our aluminum pans, raced up the steps, and rang the bell.

Esther answered the door wearing a fuzzy blue robe. "I'm so sorry," she said. "The discharge was very sudden; the hospital decided not to do the surgery until next Thursday, so they sent me home."

Plunking the food down on the kitchen counter, Michele and I both gave Esther a hug and our best wishes for a *refuah sheleimah*, and then we were off.

It was 4:30 p.m. when Michele pulled up to my house. "Enjoy the mad dash until *licht bentching*," I wished her, blowing her a quick kiss.

"You, too," she said, laughing.

"I hope we'll find out if someone ends up using our Shabbos box," I said, waving. "I'm going to email the chaplain after Shabbos and ask her to let us know. Good Shabbos!"

As I set my oven on Shabbos mode, I dreamed that the web of our mitzvah intrigue would end in a powerful explosion of beauty and transformation…

A young man in his twenties—let's call him Joey Zimmerman—is brought to the hospital just after we leave. He has fainted in the middle of an important business meeting and is showing symptoms of a concussion.

"You'll have to stay overnight," he is told by the nurse. "We need to do testing and rule out anything serious."

Joey rails at the injustice, feeling very alone as he is poked, prodded, and examined. Joey is Jewish in name only, belonging to the Reform tradition; his only real connection to Judaism is his religious grandparents, whom he views as hopelessly outdated. Still, in his low state of mind, Joey's thoughts turn to G-d.

G-d, if You truly exist, Joey thinks, staring up at the hospital TV in the room, then give me a sign.

Just then, he hears a rustling and then a knock on his door. A woman comes in holding a big box.

"Mr. Zimmerman?" she says. "My name is Chaplain Libby, and I have a Sabbath box that was just delivered for a Jewish patient. Can I leave it with you?"

Joey feels tears prick his eyes as he accepts the box. "That was quick, G-d," he murmurs, looking through the contents of his package. I think I'll give the rabbi down the block a call when I get home...

Of course, this is the first step to Joey becoming a full-fledged ba'al teshuvah...

Another scenario swept through my mind as I continued rushing through my last-minute Shabbos preparations...

A lonely old lady finds herself in the hospital. Depressed and forlorn, tears trickle down her wrinkled cheeks. No one even knows I'm here, *she thinks sadly to herself.* My husband is gone, my son lives out of state... *And then a gentle knock brings in a cheerful, smiling chaplain.*

"Mrs. Kahn?" Chaplain Libby approaches the bed. "I have a package for you."

Incredulous, Mrs. Kahn wipes her tears and takes the box. A warm feeling spreads through her heart as she examines its contents; the aching loneliness is swept away. Someone cares about me, *she thinks, smiling. She sits up straighter in bed and arranges the electric candlesticks, matzah, and grape juice on her bedside table. A light has been ignited in her eyes, the light of Shabbos and the glow of someone who feels remembered...*

5:15 p.m. Supremely grateful to be home, ready for Shabbos, and poised to light my candles, I let myself relax for a brief moment while I took a deep breath. I had trusted that Hashem would help this situation turn out as it did, but there was no denying that it had been tense and nerve-wracking for me. I said the *brachah* and the *Yehi Ratzon*, and then I added my own heartfelt words, composing yet a third possible ending to our unfinished story.

"Hashem," I said, "please take the *zechus* of this mitzvah that I did *l'shmah*. Since I didn't get the usual satisfaction from its completion, and was left with dangling question marks (like why in the world did we travel for an hour and a half to deliver food to our friend, when she was discharged and back in her home a mere few blocks from where we live?), I hope that qualifies as *l'shmah*. Please, instead of rewarding me for this mitzvah, filter the *zechus* to Menachem and Bayla Kranz, my sweet neighbors who are anxiously waiting to be blessed with children, and fill their empty arms with their hearts' desire. Enable this wonderful young couple to have children, and may they be *zocheh* to raise their children *l'Torah, l'chuppah, u'l'ma'asim tovim*."

And of course, in my mind's eye, I began dreaming of the happy conclusion that would emerge from this story nine months from now…

‑╱╲╱╲╱╲♡

JOINING THE ICU CLUB

It happened when I was on my first trip ever to Eretz Yisrael. I had gone there to help out my married daughter Yocheved, who had just given birth to her first child.

I was on my way back to Yocheved's apartment after an awesome visit to the Kosel, when my phone rang with the news that would overturn my life.

"Gavi's in the hospital," my teenage daughter said, sounding scared. "He has pneumonia and was admitted to the ICU. Tatty just called to tell us."

Immediately jolted out of my Kosel-induced serenity, I quickly called my husband, who confirmed the worrisome report. My oldest son, Gavi, who was living out of state where he had found a job, had contracted a bad case of pneumonia and was not doing well.

My mind churned. *Could this really be happening? A medical crisis? Now? When I'm so far away from everyone? It's rather incon-venient timing, isn't it?*

My husband made hurried arrangements to fly out of state to be with Gavi, and our children at home were left rudderless. Knowing that our oldest child at home, our eighteen-year-old daughter, was a responsible girl, and that she had a car and credit card at her disposal, we were fairly confident that the kids would manage in our absence. Still, the idea of both parents abandoning the fort left me feeling somewhat queasy. But it wasn't like we had much of a choice here…

Gavi had checked into the hospital before Shabbos, and within twenty-four hours, his pneumonia spiraled wildly out of control. The doctors and nurses expressed astonishment that his condition had deteriorated so rapidly, offering no logical explanation.

I wanted to jump on the next plane back to America, so I too could be at Gavi's side, but my husband told me to stay where I was. "It's not necessary for you to come," he said. "Gavi's con-dition is serious, but he's stable *baruch Hashem*, and Yocheved needs you there."

Throughout the next few tumultuous days, I was in constant touch with my husband, as well as Gavi's doctors and nurses, about Gavi's condition. Worry was my constant companion as I tried to put on a brave front and play with my baby granddaugh-ter and cook supper for my daughter; after all, it wasn't the baby or her parents' fault that the *simchah* of her birth had coincided so clashingly with this medical crisis.

The night before I returned home, I went to Kever Rochel, where I poured out my heart to Hashem. As I *davened* and cried, I felt Mama Rochel's loving arms embrace me.

"You suffered so much, Mama Rochel," I whispered. "Yet your shoulders are so broad. You hear all of your children's pain, and you carry their burdens before the Heavenly Throne and plead for comfort and an end to our endless waterfall of tears. Please ask Hashem to heal our son Gavriel…"

I swayed back and forth, allowing the emotions to surge from my heart in silent prayer. There were moments when my lips couldn't move anymore, but I knew Hashem understood my heart's desires. Finally, reluctantly, I left the holy place and prepared to return to America, to my family and my new reality: mother of a sick child.

⎯ᔕᔕᔕ♡

Almost immediately upon arriving back home, I got on another plane and flew out to be with my son Gavi in the hospital. There I joined a club that I pray will soon terminate all its participants' memberships. It is the ICU club, where people, regardless of race or creed, are united by the pain of having a loved one in grave medical condition.

People are nice here, I realized. The evening after I'd just arrived in the hospital following my long trip, I was having an altercation with a soda machine that refused to accept my dollar and grant me my soda. *Take it*, I inwardly seethed, desperately wanting my Coke Zero.

"Here," a man offered, opening his wallet and handing me a dollar.

"But I have the money," I insisted. "This machine just doesn't like me."

"Please take it," he begged, thrusting the money at me.

I understood that in this place of suffering, we club members were enjoined to help each other, to lighten one another's suffering in any way we could.

At least I'm familiar with hospitals, I naively told myself as I entered the unit. *My poor husband, on the other hand, almost never spends time in hospitals; it must have been really hard for him when he was here. But I have a medical background, both from my chaplaincy training and from being a Bikur Cholim volunteer, so I'm sure I've seen all that there is to see here.*

I've never been more wrong in my life.

Nothing could've prepared me for the sight of my child, my twenty-six-year-old baby, hooked up to a respirator, fighting for his every breath. He opened his eyes when he saw me, and they welled up with tears. My eyes spilled over in response, and we created an ocean together.

Good to see you, he wrote on his whiteboard, and I kissed him.

"Good to see you, too," I whispered, trying to smile bravely through my tears.

Gavi couldn't eat or drink, nor could he speak. He communicated by means of a dry-erase board, and the hours I spent with him were long, harrowing, and pain-filled.

I began a nightmarish kind of life, where I traveled home for a few days, spent some time with my other children, and then traveled back to Gavi to be at his side.

At one point, when I was preparing to leave home yet again to fly out to Gavi, my seven-year-old burst into tears. "Gavi sees you more than I do," she cried.

I held my daughter close. "You know, Gavi's really sick, sweetie," I told her. "He doesn't just have a cold. He's in the hospital. He needs his mommy to be there for him, very badly."

Eventually my daughter calmed down. "But if he gets better before your flight tomorrow," she directed me with a few last sniffles, "then cancel your trip, okay?"

"You got it," I replied, a sad smile playing on my lips. *Halevai,* I wished with every fiber of my being.

BARUCH HASHEM, GAVI's condition began to improve, slowly but surely. When he passed his swallow test and was allowed his first solid food in a month, even though he was still on the ventilator, the nurse brought him some applesauce. I eagerly peeled off the wrapper for him and *kvelled* as Gavi slowly ate his food.

Hashem held my hand throughout this ordeal. He connected me with an amazing family who lived in Gavi's community. This family took care of my every need, chauffeuring me to and from the hospital and serving me hot meals throughout the days of my visits. For the first time, I understood the power of *bikur cholim* from the other side, the receiving end.

How long will it be until my son is better? I wanted to know, pleading for answers from the powerful-looking men garbed in white coats.

"We can't tell you," they replied.

"Gabriel has a big blood clot," I was informed a few days later. "It will impact his breathing, so we'll need to put him back on full ventilator support."

My heart lurched at the setback; before this, they had been trying to wean Gavi completely off the ventilator!

He needed to be injected twice a day with a medication that was to help dissolve the blood clot, and I cringed whenever the nurse injected him, wincing as if the syringes were piercing my own skin.

ONE WEEK, I opted to drive the seven-hour commute to see

Gavi; other times I had gotten rides, taken a bus, or flown. A wonderful friend, Gillian, offered to do the drive with me, as I had never driven more than an hour or two on my own. Still, even with Gillian at my side as a supportive presence, I felt flutters of anxiety about the trip.

Taking a deep breath, I turned the key in the ignition and popped in a CD to soothe my nerves. To my astonishment, the following words appeared on the screen of my CD player: "*Lo L'fached* (Do Not Be Afraid)." That was the title of the first song on the CD.

Tears sprang to my eyes. "Thanks," I whispered to Hashem, hearing His reassurance loud and clear.

Midway through the drive, a warning light went on in a corner of my dashboard, informing me that my engine oil was low. I panicked and quickly turned off on the closest exit, all the while praying that my car wouldn't overheat. Two minutes later, we arrived at—would you believe it?—a body shop.

However, it was Sunday, and so the shop was closed. What to do now? we wondered.

Just then, I noticed a woman walking around outside the shop. I jumped out of my car and quickly apprised her of my situation, asking her if she could be of any help.

"We live here," she told me. "Come on in; I'll open the shop for you." She lifted the chains from around the lot and motioned me to bring my car up.

Fifteen minutes later, my car was equipped with a quart of oil, the light on the dashboard went off, and we were back on our way, marveling at the clear manifestation of *hashgachah pratis*.

Lo l'fached indeed.

After visiting Gavi, we drove back home, stopping on the way to eat lunch and *daven* Minchah. Standing outside a small store, I found myself facing a white stone wall, and memories, unbidden, filled my mind. Not long ago, I had stood in front of our holiest remnant, *our* stone wall, so close to Hashem, the closest we can approach until Mashiach comes. And now I stood in some forsaken corner of the earth, facing an oh, so different white stone wall... Yet Hashem could still hear me; He still cared what I had to say, still gathered my *tefillos* to Him.

I was mesmerized by the ribbons of gold and scarlet stretching across the darkening sky. In my small car, I made my way past graceful mountains and trees aflame in fall splendor. My heart exploded in gratitude to my Father Who was so clearly holding my hand even as I traveled this new, uncharted path in my life. Yes, this was a painfully hard time for me, and I was so ready for life to resume a normal routine again. But I was comforted that I wasn't alone as I wended my way down this long, curving road.

Over the next few weeks, Gavi's progress was slow but steady. He graduated to a regular hospital room and finally—finally!—shed the ventilator, after five endless weeks on it. For another week he received extra oxygen through his tracheotomy, while family and friends continued to storm the Heavens, begging for his full recovery.

By the end of the sixth week, Gavi was discharged from the hospital. He came home for a month to recuperate and regain his strength. *B'chasdei Hashem*, by then he was able to move back to his apartment and return to work and his regular routine.

Whenever I look at him now, I think of his wondrous recovery and thank Hashem for it all over again.

THE *CHESSED* WHEEL

SEVERAL MONTHS PASSED, and I was once again submerged in my Bikur Cholim obligations.

"Gillian called me," Michele told me one day, her voice uncharacteristically serious. "They found something on her mammogram, and she needs to have a biopsy."

I gasped. It couldn't be! The woman who had given so selflessly to me in my time of need…how could she be sick?

Immediately I called her up.

"Gillian?"

"Yes?" she answered in her melodic South African lilt.

"I've been thinking about you," I said. "How are you?"

"Funny that you should call now," she replied. And she filled me in on her medical nightmare.

"I want to take you for your biopsy," I told her, knowing that, as a widow whose grown children lived overseas, Gillian likely did not have anyone lined up to take her for the procedure.

"Oh, Rachel, that is so kind of you. Are you sure?"

"After what *you* did for *me*?" I asked. "Of course I'm sure!"

Gillian's attitude was superbly positive. "I'm sure it's nothing," she insisted as we drove together to her appointment. "I eat healthy, exercise, and have no family history of this type of cancer."

I tried to squelch the nerves tumbling inside me as I listened and prayed that she was right. It was a humbling feeling to be in a waiting room among people who were about to undergo biopsies. All of these patients were poised on a battlefield, preparing to wage a war for their lives.

Thank You, Hashem, for my health, I found myself thinking over and over again. *Please, continue to keep me away from these front lines...*

A few days later, I received a follow-up call from Gillian. "I have cancer," she told me.

My heart dropped. "Oh, Gillian," I cried out. "I'm so sorry!"

"Yes," she said. "So am I."

"What do you need?" I asked. "What can I do?"

"Well, I need to have surgery," she said. "That's the first step."

"I want to take you for it," I told her decisively.

"Are you sure?" she asked. "It's not too much for you?"

How often do we get to repay our debts in this world? I was anxious to help Gillian on two accounts: one, she was a dear friend, and I wanted to be there for her in any way I could; and two, I so badly wanted to make a small deposit in payment for the three days she'd given up for me, when she'd driven with me to visit my son Gavi. Of course, no one wants to be on the receiving end of *chessed*, but the *chessed* wheel is known to turn, and the one who so much likes to give sometimes has to take. And if Gillian was now in the position where she needed help, I wanted to be the one to give back to her.

A third reason why I wanted to help her, I realized, was because of...Mommy. The irony struck me. My own mother, too, didn't have her children at her side during her final illness. She, too, needed community support instead of a "next of kin," as her two children couldn't be with her as much as we wished; my sister and her family were living overseas in Australia at the time, and though I lived closer to my mother than that, I had six young children, with a seventh on the way, and wasn't in too mobile a position either. If I could help someone now who was in my mother's situation then, perhaps in some way I could make things up to Mommy in the *Olam Ha'Emes*...

The day of Gillian's surgery came, and my stomach churned as I drove to pick her up and bring her to the hospital. I knocked on her door, and we hugged.

"I wish we were driving out of town together again," she said. "Not for anything bad..."

"I wish I were taking you out to lunch!" I answered as we walked to my car together. Our nerves were taut, though we both tried to keep up a conversation.

Twenty minutes later, we arrived at the surgical center. It was time.

With each step we took toward the building, my fear for Gillian increased exponentially. How I wished I could take her hand and run with her, far away from this place where they would soon cut her open and make her, a seemingly healthy woman, into someone vulnerable, sick, and in pain. I found out later that Gillian's fears had also increased while climbing those stairs to the building.

We sat together and said many chapters of Tehillim, slowly, two helpless daughters entreating their Father. The timeless words bathed us in their calm, soothing waters. Dovid Hamelech had suffered greatly; he called out and was answered. *Please, Hashem*, we begged, *answer us, too.*

A nurse guided Gillian away from me so that she could be prepped for the surgery. I would be called in when she was situated in her bed.

"How are you?" I asked, sitting near her bed once she was hooked up to the IV and awaiting her turn for surgery.

"I was terrified when we first got here," she confided. "But now that I'm somewhat acclimated to where I am, I feel better. I just want it to be over with."

"Yes," I murmured. "Soon it will be behind you, and you will get on with the business of feeling better and being healthy, with Hashem's help."

A nurse popped her head in to tell Gillian, "You'll be taken into the operating theater in just a few moments."

Do they call it an operating theater because that's where a person realizes that we're all actors and actresses playing our roles in the drama called life?

"How are you holding up?" I asked Gillian. I, for one, was feeling sick at the thought of what was waiting for her.

"I'm scared," she admitted. "I just want it to be over. I hope it hasn't spread."

"With Hashem's help," I murmured. "Me, too."

Once the nurses came for her, I kissed Gillian's cheek and returned to the waiting room, where I re-opened my Tehillim and continued *davening* for her.

Overseas calls from Gillian's anxious children came through my cell phone.

"How's my mother?" they all wanted to know. But I didn't have answers yet.

Finally, a doctor came in and called out, "Family for Gillian Rosenberg?"

I nodded at her. "That would be me, I guess," I said.

The surgeon sat next to me and told me that Gillian had done well and that the tumor was out. I exhaled in relief.

"When can I see her?" I asked.

"They'll call you back when she's ready," the surgeon assured me. "We'll have the pathology results in three to five days."

Three to five days? That would be sheer torture for Gillian, all that waiting to find out if the cancer had spread, if her life was in danger—or if she would be okay! How would she manage?

I quickly filled in Gillian's anxious children about what the surgeon had shared and tried to reassure them. They were so worried.

Several days later, Gillian knew her results.

"There's good news and bad news," she began telling me, and I held my breath. I only wanted good news. "I have two forms of cancer, but they think they got it all; nothing seems to have spread. I will have to start radiation soon."

Now the long, curving road, the one I had traversed just a few months ago, belonged to Gillian...

Hashem, Merciful Father of us all, You know best what we need on our journey through this world. Give us the strength to endure, help us maintain our trust, and please, Hashem, send healing to all those who need it...

PERFECT TIMING

Bikur Cholim runs on *nissim* and *hashgachah pratis*, yet each time I'm witness to this phenomenon, it never fails to amaze me.

The other day I got an email from a volunteer who had recently undergone cancer surgery. After several months of recuperation, she wrote that she was feeling up to visiting and helping out again. I was thrilled to have her back on board, of course, and just as thrilled that she felt well enough to resume her normal activities.

Shortly after reading that email, my phone rang.

"Hi, Rachel," Shoshie, a friend of mine, greeted me. "I'm going to have to cancel the ride I was supposed to give Suzie on Friday. I'm really sorry, but something just came up and I won't be able to do it."

"No problem," I said. "I'll take care of it."

"Are you sure? You'll be able to find someone else to pick up Suzie from her appointment?"

"Yup," I said. "Don't worry about it."

I quickly sent an email to my reinstated volunteer.

Yes, she wrote back. *I am available this Friday and am happy to help.*

If that's not *hashgachah pratis*, I don't know what is!

RABBI, YOU GOTTA HAVE FAITH!

The news of the illness of a young *rebbi* in our community, the father of a large family, sent shock waves through us all. Renal failure? Rabbi Sheinerman? How could it be? I pictured the young, vibrant man and couldn't connect him with the word *illness* and all that it involved.

Bikur Cholim reached out, and it became my job to set up a system of transportation for Rabbi Sheinerman, to help him get to and from dialysis three times a week. With Hashem's help, I found men eager to take on this mitzvah and help this special person.

"I have to thank you, Mrs. Stein," one of the volunteers told me one Shabbos when we met on the street. "I have learned so much from these rides with Rabbi Sheinerman. We talk Torah the whole time, and I have gained immeasurably from it."

My heart swelled. How beautiful for a volunteer to thank *me*. It can't get much better than that.

Rabbi Sheinerman's situation, though, was not getting better at all; week by week, he was growing weaker and frailer, and his black beard became tinged with silver. He was in urgent need of a new kidney, but despite intensive efforts, a match had still not been found for him. The community was frightened, and we all kept him in our daily *tefillos*.

Then at last, good news came: Rabbi Sheinerman's oldest brother, Baruch, was a perfect match! Several of Rabbi Sheinerman's brothers had vied for the privilege of donating their kidney to their brother, but Baruch, as the oldest, was given priority. He flew into town for more testing, and a surgery date was set.

And then, at the last minute, Rabbi Sheinerman received the dreaded call.

"Some of your brother's test results came back as incompatible with yours," the nurse said. "He won't be able to give you his kidney, after all."

Our hearts fell alongside those of the Sheinerman family, and our *tefillos* intensified. Many people accepted upon themselves to recite *Asher Yatzar* with more *kavanah*, realizing the tremendous gift inherent in working kidneys.

Rabbi Sheinerman told us that he got that call while in middle of undergoing dialysis, and his first reaction was to begin crying.

Throughout the months of his treatment, Rabbi Sheinerman had become the unofficial rabbi of the group of dialysis patients in the hospital with him, encouraging the others who had lost their will to live.

"You gotta have faith," he would tell them. "G-d is good."

But when his own hopes were dashed so stunningly, he couldn't help it, and tears of helplessness and hopelessness dripped onto his beard.

A large black woman, also a dialysis patient, noticed and approached him.

"Rabbi, what's wrong?" she asked. "Why are you crying?"

He told her.

"Rabbi!" she exclaimed. "You told us you gotta have faith! Come on, Rabbi! Where's your faith?"

Well, several other of Rabbi Sheinerman's brothers were tested and rejected at the last minute, similar to what happened the first time around, and we all collectively held our breaths while watching helplessly as Rabbi Sheinerman continued to deteriorate.

Finally, another brother, Yosef, was found to be a match, and once again, a surgery date was arranged. *Baruch Hashem*, Yosef's subsequent testing came out to be fine, and the surgery went ahead as planned. Tehillim booklets were set up in the home of a friend, and we took turns stopping by and saying them, begging Hashem that all should go well for Rabbi Sheinerman.

When I called Mrs. Sheinerman after the surgery to find out how it had gone, her tears of happiness were evident over the phone.

"He has a working kidney!" she cried. "*Mah rabu ma'asecha, Hashem* (How great are Your works, Hashem)!"

And I cried joyfully along with her, too.

But that isn't the end of the story. While Rabbi Sheinerman's oldest brother Baruch had been in town undergoing testing, he had noticed a *bachur* there who made a favorable impression on him. Just a few weeks after the surgery, mazel tovs resounded, and once again, we were awed: Baruch Sheinerman's daughter was engaged to that very *bachur* from our community! The *kallah's* father had been rejected as a donor, but Hashem had His reasons for bringing him to town anyway...

MY STUDENTS, MY TEACHERS

For several years, I had the unique privilege of teaching *Chumash* to a lively group of seniors. Their insight, candidness, and humor made that hour I spent with them the highlight of my week. And though they called themselves my students, these seniors really became my teachers, as I learned so much from them.

I only began teaching them because of Chaya. "I know you're busy," she had said to me one day, "and it's probably silly of me to even ask you. But we're looking for someone to teach *Chumash* to our group once a week, and we thought of you."

When I called her back the next day to say yes, I would be happy to teach them, Chaya was overjoyed. And that was the beginning of my wonderful relationship with this special woman, a relationship that I will always remember and cherish.

Diminutive in stature, Chaya was a giant in spirit. At seventy-plus, she had the energy of someone at least twenty years younger. She was bright, spunky, and had an unconditional love for everyone she met. As a *ba'alas teshuvah*, she had a passionate desire to grow and learn, desperately trying to make up for lost time. Although teachers should never have favorites, I admit that Chaya had that special something about her that wormed its way into my heart right from the very start. She was like the *bubby* I'd never had. Each time she called me "*Mammele*," I melted.

We talked, we analyzed, we learned, and we laughed. Our classroom, Chaya's dining room, was a safe place where any question or comment was worthy. I loved the classes, and it seemed that all the participants did, too.

But then Chaya was diagnosed with pancreatic cancer, and our classes took on a more serious tone. We became soldiers on a battlefield, fighting for Chaya's life with whatever merits we had. We *davened* for her every day and dedicated our learning for her recovery. Additionally, each of us took on a private resolve to do something extra in her *zechus*, hoping to tip the scales and avert a bad decree. Yet despite our valiant efforts, Hashem, in His wisdom, had a different plan, and we watched our dear friend fading before our eyes.

One afternoon, when the end seemed close, I came to Chaya's bedside. Shaken by her wasted appearance, I greeted her lovingly, craving her typical warmth in return. But Chaya's eyes had lost their sparkle, and she stared right through me, seeming not to recognize me. I forced myself to hold back my tears. Where was my "*bubby*"? What had become of my special friend?

Another friend from our group, Faiga, was there at the time, and we walked out of the room together.

"She doesn't recognize me," I whispered, feeling a jagged rip in my heart.

"It doesn't matter," Faiga replied, with trademark candidness. "All that matters is that she knows there are people surrounding her who love her. Whether she knows us or not is irrelevant."

And I thought I knew how to perform *bikur cholim*. Here was Faiga, my student, teaching me a lesson that would stay with me forever. I wanted a return on my investment. I craved recognition and the magical feeling I got from being Chaya's special friend and adopted granddaughter. Faiga, though, in her humility, wanted nothing in return. She simply wanted Chaya to feel comfortable and loved. Hers was a real *chessed*, a *chessed shel emes*.

I wondered if I would ever reach Faiga's level. I doubted it, but I hoped that if I continued to teach these *neshei chayil* long enough, maybe I would eventually learn to emulate their sterling ways.

DOUBLE HEADER

"Did you hear what happened?" A white-faced friend pulled me aside after a girls' play, and I could see and feel Sara Leah's urgency. "The Goldmans' fifth-grade daughter, Chevi, was walking home yesterday, and she got hit by a car."

"Chevi Goldman?" I gasped. "Is she okay?"

"She had a concussion and she broke some ribs," Sara Leah told me. "One of her ankles might also be broken; I'm not sure. Hopefully she'll be okay, *b'ezras Hashem*; she just needs time to heal."

"*Oy!*" I said. "I'll call her mother and see what we can do." I imagined this young girl walking unsuspectingly home from school when, in a heartbeat, all normalcy turned on its head and she was rushed to the hospital. *But at least she'll be okay,* b'ezras Hashem, I consoled myself.

"It gets worse," Sara Leah continued quietly.

I waited, holding my breath, not sure I wanted to hear.

"Nosson Gutman was the driver."

I felt the blood drain from my face. Nosson Gutman was one of the sweetest people I knew. He was always doing things for other people; I don't think the word "I" existed in his vocabulary. A retired doctor, he devoted his days to attending *shiurim* and doing *chessed*.

Oh, that poor, poor man… I thought to myself. My heart went out to him.

"He was actually taking someone home from the hospital when it happened," Sara Leah said. "I think he needs some support."

I wasn't sure who I felt worse for: Chevi and her family, who were now enmeshed in a medical crisis; or Nosson, who had caused all this pain—albeit accidentally—and now had to live with himself.

When I got home, I called the Goldmans to offer *bikur cholim* assistance. They said that once Chevi was able to return to school, they would appreciate help getting her there and home, since both parents worked. I told them it shouldn't be a problem to work that out.

Then my husband and I together made the harder call, and we went over to Nosson Gutman's house.

"I don't know if I ever want to drive again," Nosson confided to us as we sat near him in his living room. "I know that everything comes from Hashem, but to think I was responsible for this…" His eyes filled and spilled over, and mine did, too. My husband squeezed his hand, but we had no words of comfort to offer.

"I'm so sorry," I murmured. "To think such a thing could happen to you, such a special person… It's just too much to comprehend."

"I need to grieve," he said. "I'm in such agony now, and I'm going to need time to process my pain… *Oy*, I'll feel so much better when I know Chevi is back on her feet."

My heart was heavy when we finally got up to leave. And I *davened* that both Chevi and Nosson should have a *refuah she-leimah*, and that we should only hear *besuros tovos* from then on.

Chevi had a long and drawn-out recovery. But with each step of progress that she made, Nosson seemed to brighten a shade, and he returned a little more to his old self.

It took some time, but *baruch Hashem*, Chevi is now once again an active and healthy girl, completely healed from her injuries. And finally, with Hashem's help, Nosson is back to his job of being a solid and confident pillar in our community.

SETTING BOUNDARIES

OVER THE YEARS, I think we've managed to take most Bikur Cholim requests in stride. But there was one situation that spiraled out of control, and it taught me some really important lessons—namely, in how to set boundaries.

His name was Steve Farber, and he was a fifty-five-year-old bachelor. With no family other than a handicapped sister who lived in a local nursing home, Steve adopted our community as his family. Fiercely independent, he worked hard as a mental health counselor in a group practice.

But then Steve got into a car accident in which he injured his leg. He sheepishly admitted that he had been driving after not sleeping an entire night and had fallen asleep at the wheel.

"I was up all night reviewing a client's case," he explained to me frankly when I came to visit him. "I guess it was too much for my body to handle... It's a miracle I wasn't hurt worse."

"That's for sure. Tell me, how can we help you?"

He asked us to arrange rides for him to get to and from his appointments. Little did we know that this was just the beginning...

"And who's going to visit my sister, Annie?" He lifted his guileless blue eyes to me, and now his tone sounded more like a demand than a question. "I normally visit her every day, you know, and now, of course, I won't be able to. Will you be able to arrange visitors for her, Mrs. Stein?"

I gulped. Arranging transportation for Steve Farber's regular weekly appointments, for the unforeseeable future, would be a big job in and of itself, especially considering the limited pool of volunteers that is available in a community as small as ours. Couple that with—did he say *daily?*—visits to his sister on the other side of town, and, well, you can understand my feeling of being overloaded.

"Mr. Farber," I said meekly, "we may be able to send a *weekly* visitor to your sister. We'll try our best, but with our limited amount of volunteers, we can't make promises... I hope you can understand."

But I don't think he did, as his requests, or rather demands, kept on coming. He wanted meals from us, he wanted someone to take him to do his errands, and, when he felt a bit better, he wanted to be driven to and from work each day.

Then he asked if someone could come and keep him company for the rest of the time, when he wasn't doing anything.

"I need help," he confided. "I'm a people person, and I need to be with people. I go crazy when I'm by myself. I'm lonely, but I just can't get out the way I usually do, because of my condition. Doesn't anyone care?!"

Yes, Steve, I felt like saying, *we do care. But we have our own lives, too, and there are others who are relying on us, as well. We're only human, and there's only so much we are capable of doing...* But of course I couldn't say that to him, and so I just swallowed hard and we continued twisting ourselves into pretzels in an effort to help him with his needs.

Steve's recuperation took a very long time. Each time we thought he was almost back to himself, and we were about to heave an inward sigh of relief, he re-injured yet another vertebrae and was back in patient mode again, with more incessant demands of Bikur Cholim.

"Methinks it's time for him to hire some help," I said to Michele one day. "I can't deal with this anymore. He's not the only one who calls Bikur Cholim for help, and it's just too much."

"I agree," Michele said. "Do you want to be the one to tell him this, though?"

"Um…"

When the next slew of demands poured in from Steve, I understood why Hashem wanted women to cover their hair. "It's to prevent them from pulling it out in situations like these," I told Michele with sage-like wisdom, and we laughed. Then I heard my call-waiting beep, and I checked the number. Need I have checked? Of course it was Steve Farber…

Michele called me a few days later. "Steve wants a meeting with us," she said. "He said he needs more help."

"Arghh!" I yelped, massaging my temples.

"I couldn't have said it better myself," Michele said. "I arranged to meet with him at seven this evening. Is that good for you? Can I pick you up then?"

"You might have to really pick me up," I mumbled. "Because I, for one, feel like I have no more energy for this…"

That's when Michele and I both decided that enough was enough. What was going on here had entirely left the parameters of the concept of *chessed*, and we simply couldn't cope like this anymore. Right then and there, we resolved that while meeting with Steve Farber that evening, we would come prepared with a speech of our own. We would tell him that while we were still determined to help him in whatever way we could, there were certain non-negotiable boundaries that we had to set down, for our sake and for the sake of the whole Bikur Cholim organization.

Need I tell you that Steve Farber was *not* happy to hear our new stipulations? For quite a while, he ranted and raved about it. "Is this how a *chessed* organization acts?!" he railed. "You make me *hire* and *pay* for someone to help me out, instead of extending help to an injured man?!"

We felt terrible hearing his accusations, but we held our ground. There was just no other way.

I learned a lot from this difficult experience. Firstly, it taught me patience, as I had to reach deep within my reserves of that *middah* when dealing with Steve Farber. Secondly, I learned about the importance of setting boundaries. Every person has his or her limitations, and if he/she refuses to acknowledge those limitations, everyone ends up suffering.

⌇⌇⌇♡

DON'T FALL!

Funny how extraordinary things happen when you least expect them.

I was in the grocery store for the second time in twenty-four hours, planning to run in and out for that one item I had neglected to get the first time around. It was then that I saw her: Helene, one of the elderly people whom I call on Fridays to wish "good Shabbos." She was shopping together with Shevi Roth, a giant-hearted woman in the community who is one of my Bikur Cholim volunteers.

My eyes grew round with admiration. Although I enjoy visiting the elderly, shopping with them—at least when I need to get my own shopping done, too—is an altogether different story. Grocery shopping is one of my least favorite activities. Tie that together with doubling or tripling the amount of time in the store, and voila: a recipe doomed for disaster.

As I was pondering this *tzaddekes* of a woman who was slowing her steps for Helene, I spotted another of my elderly friends, Raizel, in a different aisle. I knew that Raizel had recently given up driving, so obviously someone had given her a ride to the store… It didn't take long to figure it out: Shevi had taken both Helene and Raizel shopping with her!

Wow, I thought, suddenly feeling envious of Shevi's enormous *zechus. I wish I could do this kind of* chessed…

I left the store, still craving the opportunity to do a *chessed* of such magnitude. And, unbelievably enough, as I walked outside, I beheld a situation that Hashem must have designed just so that I, too, should be able to do a *chessed* right now.

An old man was pushing a shopping cart, but his legs were buckling, and it looked like he would collapse on the floor at any moment. A man who appeared to be his helper was trying his best to hold him up from behind and prevent him from falling, but he looked like he was losing the battle. I immediately dropped my pocketbook behind me on the ground and rushed forward, grabbing hold of the old man from one side, using all of my strength to hold him up. He was limp, like a rag doll, and his body kept sliding down toward the hard cement. I met the eyes of his helper on the other side, and we both clutched tighter. I could feel my arms quivering as every muscle strained to fight against letting this old man fall to the ground.

"Can someone drive up to meet him?" I panted, wondering how in the world we would get him to his car all the way out in the parking lot when we could barely even get him to the edge of the sidewalk now.

"His wife is bringing the car," the helper gasped.

I tried to encourage the old man. "One foot in front of the other," I said. "Baby steps. You can do it."

But his legs, or maybe it was his mind, refused to cooperate. So the helper and I each tried to coax a leg into taking a step, all the while holding strong to his upper body so that he wouldn't buckle and fall.

"Someone's pocketbook?" a black worker called out, lifting my pocketbook from the ground.

"Mine," I panted. "Thanks."

It took about ten minutes until we were able to shuffle the man to where his wife had pulled up their car, about four or five feet away. When we finally helped him get situated in the car, everyone breathed sighs of relief.

The old man's wife came up to me and hugged me, tears in her eyes. "Thank you," she whispered.

"It's okay," I told her. I felt the pain and fear emanating from her very being. I imagined her thinking, *What happened to my big, strong husband? He used to take care of me, and now—this. I'm not ready for this, and I don't know how to handle it. Why is getting old so excruciatingly difficult…?*

I didn't have answers for her, although I wished she didn't have to go through this. As I bade her a warm farewell, a *tefillah* rose up from my heart: *Please, Hashem, let me stay healthy and never become dependent and infirm in my old age…*

The black worker was still there, holding my pocketbook for me. "If I'd been there first," he quipped, flashing a white grin, "I would've just picked him up like this and carried him to the car." He held his hands out in a cradle position, the way one would carry a baby.

"You should have," I said, smiling back at him and taking my pocketbook from his hand. *But I'm glad you didn't, because then I wouldn't have had this opportunity to help.*

As I walked to my car, gratitude surged within me. How marvelous to be able to stride through a parking lot on my own two feet! What a gift!

And thank You, Hashem, for turning a simple shopping trip into a special *chessed* opportunity for me.

⌁⌁⌁♡

PRAYER IS NEVER FOR NOTHING

"You probably heard," Dena began after hearing my voice, "that I have a tumor."

I had heard. That was actually why I called. But I couldn't help it; I gasped anyway. To hear her say it straight out like that somehow made it very real and terribly frightening.

"It's probably benign…"

"Phew!" I broke in. "*Baruch Hashem*, that's good."

"But I have to go to a surgeon," she went on. "Apparently, some tumors just need to be watched, while others have to be surgically removed. The surgeon will decide whether or not this tumor needs to be removed. Of course I'm hoping for the first option."

"Me, too," I breathed.

Dena sighed. "I also have Henry on my head now." Henry was Dena's older brother, and she was his caregiver. "It's time for them to put in Henry's new stent; his old one is not working, and he keeps having setbacks because of it. But it's not simple. The doctor said that he might not survive the surgery, and even if he does, he might become a vegetable.

"Now, I like vegetables," Dena quipped, "but not in place of my brother. So I don't know what to do. Oh, and his cancer has metastasized. The doctor gave him three months. Rachel, what would you do about the surgery?"

Me? You want me to handle a life and death question? What do I know? I do have a fear of operating on elderly people, especially knowing Henry's history. He already had two heart attacks, and he recently recovered from pneumonia. And the doctor doesn't sound too optimistic about performing the surgery on him…

"Dena, I can tell you my gut feeling, but you have to speak with a doctor and your rabbi. I have no medical knowledge whatsoever."

"Okay," she prodded me on.

"I would be afraid of putting him through surgery at his age and in his condition. You said yourself that the doctor thinks he might not survive the surgery, and if he does, he might become a vegetable. So it sounds like it might hasten things…" I trailed off, saddened by what she was going through.

"Yes, I'm leaning toward that feeling also. At first, I was going to leave it up to Henry to decide. But now I'm thinking he shouldn't have the surgery, so maybe I don't want to leave it up to him to decide… And who is the doctor, anyway, to tell me how long Henry has to live? Is he G-d? No one but G-d knows when Henry's time will come."

"You're right."

"I'm also worried," Dena continued. "If I have to have surgery, who's going to take care of Henry?" Another sigh. "Anyway, Rachel, tell me: are there any special prayers I should say for him?"

"Well, Tehillim always helps," I offered.

"I'm a little afraid of Tehillim," Dena confided. "Any time I've ever been in a Tehillim group, the person we *davened* for died. So I feel like it doesn't work."

Oh, boy… "Dena," I said softly. "There's no such thing as an unanswered prayer. You can say whatever prayer you want—and you should know that Tehillim *is* most definitely effective—but we humans never know what Hashem does with the prayers we say. Sometimes He prolongs a patient's life because of them; sometimes He eases the person's suffering; sometimes the prayers help out the person's descendants. So even if, unfortunately, the patient you pray for dies, you should know that your prayers and Tehillim are *never* for nothing. They're always doing *something* good for the person."

There was a moment of silence. Then, "So who do I give Henry's name to? Who runs the Tehillim group now?"

Thatta girl, Dena! I silently congratulated her, breathing a sigh of relief. *I knew you had that* emunah *within you the whole time…*

〰️♡

DID I START AN EPIDEMIC?!

IT WAS ONE of those short winter Erev Shabbosos again. As far as Bikur Cholim needs, I didn't foresee any; I had put in my time this week and expected to plunge headlong into Shabbos preparations the moment I came home from my exercise class.

On my way to the gym, I called Shani, whose father, Mr. Shuman, was in the hospital. "Hi, Shani. Just checking in to see how your father is doing."

"Oh, thanks for calling, Rachel—and thank you so much for sending him visitors yesterday!" Shani gushed. "He was so happy!"

"I'm glad," I said, feeling a surge of satisfaction.

"But I was wondering," Shani continued, and I felt my insides tense up as I tried to think what I would do if she needed something from Bikur Cholim before Shabbos, "do you think anyone can visit him over Shabbos?"

Hmm, that didn't sound too difficult. I thought for a moment, and then—bingo!—came up with one idea.

"I can call the Borensteins for you. They just moved to that area of town, where the hospital is. I'll take care of that."

"Yeah, that would be so nice. Just so he shouldn't be alone for the entire Shabbos."

"Okay. I'll get on it."

I was really not planning to put major effort into this situation. It was Erev Shabbos, after all, and I was having company, too. *Just one call*, I told myself. *That's all you need to do for this.*

But that one call soon turned into many. There was no answer at the Borensteins', so I left a message on both their home machine and cell phone. Then the name of someone else who lived in that area popped into my head. When I called her, she said she wouldn't be able to go, but she gave me a few more ideas of people to try.

Sigh. By the time I finished making ten calls, leaving messages on everyone's voice mails, while simultaneously trying to do my cooking, forty-five minutes had whizzed by.

Get that chicken in the oven, Rachel—quick! Peel those potatoes! Chop those vegetables!

Somehow, I made it to Shabbos with all of my cooking done. All throughout Shabbos, I wondered if anyone had heard my messages and had actually gone to visit Mr. Shuman in the hospital.

Over Motza'ei Shabbos and Sunday, a few people called me back:

"I'm sorry, Rachel. Something unexpected came up, and I couldn't get over to visit him…"

"I didn't get your message until after Shabbos."

Were all of my efforts for naught, then? I had really wanted Mr. Shuman to have visitors. And, I'll admit it, I also wanted to see fruits from my labors. After all, it hadn't been easy for me to make all those calls on such a hectic Erev Shabbos.

That evening, I called Shani to find out how her father was doing. If I was sending visitors to him, I needed to know when he was going to be discharged.

"He's doing better, *baruch Hashem*," she said. "Rachel, the Wassers visited him on Shabbos. My father was so thrilled. He said an entire family came, parents, kids—it made his day. Did you call them?"

I exhaled and felt a blooming bubble of satisfaction well up within me. "Yup, I did. Good—I am really glad it worked out."

Was I ever!

But maybe I'd patted myself a little too heartily on the back, because just a few days later, I found myself in what appeared to be an ocean of hot water.

It began when I bumped into Ellie Stengel and casually mentioned to her that Mr. Shuman was still in the hospital and in need of visitors.

"But I just spoke with his daughter Shani," she told me, her eyes wide with blazing exclamation points. "She said her father has pneumonia, and that no one should go visit him!"

I caught my breath. Uh-oh. This was trouble. I had just emailed two would-be visitors this morning, and for all I knew, they had already gone to visit Mr. Shuman. Would I now be responsible for exposing them to a contagious illness and, *chas v'shalom*, making them seriously sick? I gulped hard. And then, if the germs spread further… My nightmare mushroomed, as did my confusion. Why hadn't Shani said anything to me about this?

"Shani didn't tell me," I said lamely, shaking my head incredulously.

"Well, she told me," Ellie said. "I'm telling you the truth."

"Oh, I believe you," I assured her. "It's just that I sent people to go visit him, and now I'm feeling kind of concerned…"

Oh, boy… Why, oh, why, hadn't Shani told me this information? How could she have put me in this kind of position? My confusion gradually gave way to anger.

I tried to give Shani the benefit of the doubt. *Now, now, Rachel,* I told myself. *The poor lady works full-time and is trying to attend to her family and her father singlehandedly. She probably just forgot.*

But that's irresponsible! another side of me tried arguing back.

No, it's human. You wouldn't have done any better.

As soon as I could, I called Shani and asked her, point-blank, what the latest was with her father.

"He has pneumonia," she told me. Then she added, "You know, at first it sounded like he was too contagious to have visitors, but don't worry—the doctors assured me that as long as the visitors gown up, it should be fine for them to come. I was really happy to hear that, because we all know how much he loves visitors…"

I felt the weight of the world lift from my shoulders. Phew! What a relief! At least I hadn't started an epidemic in the community. Imagine how busy Bikur Cholim would have been then!

-ƛ┐∿┤┐∿┤┐∿♡

UNTANGLING THE KNOTS

JUST WHEN I think I have *bikur cholim* down pat, that this is the mitzvah that I have cornered and know inside out, Hashem reminds me how much more I still have to learn.

"Rachel, my mother's in the hospital." Chani sounded breathless. "I just got back from out of town, and I can't take any more time off from work. Do you think you can get her some visitors? She's in the ICU, but she's doing somewhat better. I would love for her to have some company."

I quickly sent out an email to about ten potential visitors. And then my friend Shuli and I hustled to the hospital to see Mrs. Klein.

The visit started with an unplanned tour of the hospital. Just as we got to her room in the ICU, we were informed that she was in the process of being transferred to a different room, in a regular ward. We scooted down the hall and up to the new room, but the nurses there claimed that they didn't have any Mrs. Klein coming to the room number we gave them. So we tapped our feet and waited, and finally, after extensive detective work, they found her.

Down we trooped to a different floor. "No need for the gym today," I said wryly to Shuli, as we both tried to catch our breath. A few minutes later, we were knocking on Mrs. Klein's door.

Mrs. Klein burst into tears when she saw us. She was feeling down, lonely, and tired of being sick.

"And my hair!" she moaned, reaching out to touch her hair, which hung in tangled, unruly waves around her face. "Just look at how awful it is."

Should I offer to help her with her hair? I wondered, knowing there was probably a brush somewhere in my pocketbook. *But what about germs?* I wavered. *I guess I can always wash the brush, but still...*

We stayed for a short while, trying our best to encourage Mrs. Klein and tell her that she was certainly making progress; after all, she was now out of the ICU and in a regular ward! Then we wished her a sincere *refuah sheleimah* and left the room.

When we got to the elevator, Shuli stopped and looked at me. "I bet they have combs at the nurses' station," she said. With raised eyebrows, I followed her back in the direction we had come.

Sure enough, a nurse was more than happy to provide Shuli with a comb.

We stepped back into Mrs. Klein's room. "Guess what, Mrs. Klein?" Shuli said, brandishing the comb like a prize. "I got a comb, and now I can do your hair!"

She lovingly approached the elderly lady and began to comb out Mrs. Klein's disheveled silvery locks. I watched, awed by the *chessed* Shuli was doing, and I kicked myself for not having taken that initiative myself.

You saw the need. You knew she felt uncomfortable about her hair, but you didn't act on it. Shuli, on the other hand, acknowledged the opportunity AND pounced on it. I envied Shuli's *zechus,* and imagined that with each knot she untangled, another mitzvah scurried up to *Shamayim* to be deposited in her account.

Ah, well. I sighed. *I'll file this lesson away for next time.*

"You really made her feel good," I told Shuli as we got in the elevator a few minutes later. "I thought of doing it, but you actually did it. Beautiful."

"She cares very much about her appearance," Shuli replied simply. "She needs to be neat and put together in order to feel good about herself."

WEAK EYESIGHT, STRONG VISION

ROBIN WAS HOME recovering from eye surgery. I called her to ask if she was up to visitors.

"I would love for you to come!" she exclaimed. So we made a date and the next Tuesday morning, off I went to her house.

"How are you managing?" I asked her.

"Doing a little better each day," she told me. "But I'm impatient. I want to be back to my regular life already. I don't like being dependent and stuck at home."

"I don't blame you," I sympathized. "It's hard when you can't go about your normal routine. Hopefully soon…"

"What's hardest for me to handle right now is my son's new diagnosis," she shared, and her expression clouded over. "He's twenty-two." She hesitated. "And he was just diagnosed with MS."

"Oh, Robin! I'm so sorry."

"But you know something? He's doing better than I am about it. He's determined to conquer this, and to finish pharmaceutical school. So he's been in the hospital for a week, doing all kinds of therapies and trying different types of medications. When they release him, he'll be going to a day program and doing therapy. And they said by next month, he should be able to go back to school."

"Wow," I murmured. "*Baruch Hashem.*"

"What's amazing is his attitude," she continued. "He's not letting this get him down. It's just a blip on the screen for him, and he plans to get past it. Honestly, I'm having a harder time with it than he is."

"Of course," I said. "You're his mother."

I thought of a woman I know whose MS had robbed her of all normalcy and had transformed her from a brilliant, successful professor into a dependent invalid. I shuddered, hoping Robin's son had a different strain of MS, or that doctors and researchers had made progress in their ability to treat the disease.

"What do the doctors say?" I asked, afraid to hear the prognosis.

"They think they can get him into remission."

"That's great! *Halevai.*"

"Yes. So this," here Robin gestured to her bandage-covered eye, "is nothing. I know it will get better. And the truth is, even with what my son is going through, I know there's a lot to be grateful for. His friends have been amazing. They've been going to visit him, and they told him that when he goes back to school, they'll help him. Isn't that nice?"

Wow, I thought. *Here is a woman whose eyesight may presently be weak, but boy, does she know how to view a cup as half full rather than half empty!*

By the time I left, I knew Robin had given me much more than I had given her. She'd provided me with the reminder that waking up healthy each morning is a gift, something not to be taken for granted. And she'd sent me the unspoken message that if people can overcome real challenges with optimism, fortitude, and trust, then how could anyone—myself included—let traffic jams or long supermarket lines get them down?

MOUNTAINS AND VALLEYS

Two STINGING SLAPS were delivered to our community within the span of a few days. Mr. Rabinowitz, a middle-aged man, a normal, healthy husband and father in our community, fell, broke his neck, and wound up in the ICU. To compound matters, he developed pneumonia soon afterward. Suffice it to say, he was in pretty bad shape.

When news of what had happened spread, people walked around in a state of horrified shock. Mr. Rabinowitz's name—Yaakov ben Chaya Esther—became a fixture on our lips during that time, as we begged Hashem to send him a *refuah sheleimah*.

"What can we do to help out?" we asked Mr. Rabinowitz's wife.

All she requested was help with meals; her mother was coming in to take care of the children.

As so often happens in these kinds of situations, I got a glimpse of the specialness of Klal Yisrael; my phone began to ring off the hook, with offers for help pouring in. I didn't have to make one phone call to ask for a meal; so many people offered of their own accord that all I had to do was simply organize the dates. Truly, *Mi k'amcha Yisrael!*

As soon as Mr. Rabinowitz's condition had stabilized, he was rushed into surgery. *Baruch Hashem*, the surgery was successful, but he still had a long road ahead of him.

And then we received more bad news. Our friend, a cancer survivor who had been in remission for a number of years, had a recurrence; her disease was back. Many of us felt physically ill when we heard about it. We were asked to *daven*…so we did.

"I'm so sorry," I told her. "Please, tell me, what can we do for you?"

"I don't need anything," she assured me. "My kids are older now, and I have friends who can drive me for treatments. I just want your *tefillos*, that's all."

I assured her that I would definitely give her that, and I offered her my heartfelt *brachah* for a restoration to good health.

That night I got ready to attend my friend's daughter's *sheva brachos*. It was a very big *simchah*, as the girl was "older," having been in the *parshah* of *shidduchim* for a while before meriting to find her *bashert*.

That's the way life is, I mused, checking my make-up and fastening my necklace on my way out to the *simchah*. There are ups and downs, mountains and valleys. The kindness of Hashem is that even when we are deep down in a low valley, we can still see the shining sun and use it to find our way over to the next mountain and up to its peak.

〰️

A "RUFF" DAY

I HAD JUST walked in to visit an elderly widow when my cell phone rang.

It was the secretary from our shul. "Rachel, can you find

someone to pick up Leon Ross's son from the airport tomorrow?"

My heart sank. This wasn't a Bikur Cholim request; it was a regular *chessed* one. Granted, Leon Ross wasn't your typical self-sufficient person who could be expected to drive to the airport himself to pick up his adult son; he was an unfortunate and needy kind of fellow, who was always requesting favors from others. But still, how could I bother my dedicated Bikur Cholim volunteers for something like this? If we were to take on *chessed* requests like this all the time, in addition to our many Bikur Cholim ones, we wouldn't have a moment to breathe!

You know what? I told myself. *Don't think about this right now. You're here to visit Mrs. Silverberg—give her your all. When you get home, you'll figure out what you'll do about this situation.*

The visit was pleasant enough, but all too soon I was driving home, my mind awhirl with different ways of dealing with Leon's situation. Could I consider Leon a *choleh*, in which case I could present the request to my volunteers as just another Bikur Cholim need? I mean, technically speaking, Leon was sick with a bad case of food poisoning at the moment (I had found this out from the shul secretary), so it wouldn't really be a lie, right?

Come on, Rachel, give me a break. It's just an upset stomach, and whoever knows Leon Ross will know this. You can't play games with your Bikur Cholim volunteers like that.

Okay, so that probably wouldn't work... Next idea: maybe I could hire a taxi or transportation agency to pick up his son, and I'd pay for it using our Bikur Cholim fund? *Oh, but I can't use our fund if it's not Bikur Cholim...*

I hashed out the situation with two friends of mine, but was still no closer to knowing what to do. I decided it was time to call our *rav*.

"This qualifies as *chessed*, not *bikur cholim*," he pronounced.

"So then I can't use our fund to hire a driver," I said, disappointed.

The *rav's* next words astounded me, and I marveled at his sensitivity and wisdom: "Nevertheless, it does sound like this man needs Bikur Cholim's help, even if technically he's not a *choleh*. I think Bikur Cholim *should* help him out by hiring a driver for him, and since hiring a driver will save your organization from burnout, you would be allowed to use your Bikur Cholim fund for it."

I breathed a sigh of relief, thanked him, and then began making calls to transportation agencies. That's when I realized I didn't even know what time Leon's son would be arriving.

I quickly called Leon.

"Hi, this is Rachel Stein from Bikur Cholim," I said. "We're working on arranging a driver to pick up your son from the airport tomorrow. What time is his flight arriving?"

"Oh, I just hired someone to pick him up," Leon said blithely. "It's going to cost me a lot of money, you know, but it was taking you too long to get back to me, and I couldn't wait anymore."

Biting my lip, I tried doing some deep breathing exercises as my mental Rolodex rewound to each phone call I had just made, including the busy *rav*.

But Leon wasn't finished talking.

"You know, my wife is having a procedure done on Monday," he said. "The doctors say she could possibly have a stroke on the operating table. But without the procedure, she can't eat—she's in too much pain. I authorized them to do it, but I'm scared. If anything happens to her, I'll never forgive myself."

Omigoodness... Maybe Leon never really needed the airport run altogether. Maybe all he needed was an ear...

"We'll *daven*," I told him. "Your wife should have a *refuah sheleimah*."

Drained, I hung up the phone—only to have it ring soon after. It was one of my volunteers, calling to tell me that she couldn't visit a patient in the hospital the next day as planned.

"My dog was just diagnosed with rheumatoid arthritis," she choked, "and we have to go to the rheumatologist tomorrow. He's in so much pain...my tears just keep coming..."

"I'm so sorry," I said, trying to be with her in her pain.

It had been a "ruff" day.

$$\sim\!\!\!\!\!\!\sim\!\!\!\!\!\!\sim\!\!\!\heartsuit$$

TYING UP LOOSE ENDS

PEACEFULLY MAKING POTATO kugel one Thursday night, I was humming along with the CD that was playing when the phone rang.

"Hi, Rachel. This is Shira Weiner. We're in the airport now, on our way to New York, and my father-in-law was just taken to the hospital. Can you find someone to stay with him?"

My heart began hammering. My married son and his family from out of town, whom I rarely see, were coming for a visit this Shabbos and were due to arrive within the hour. Did I have time to make phone calls now?

"I'll see what I can do," I assured Shira, taking down the information she gave me. *How in the world am I going to do this?* I wondered, but I pulled out my trusty directory and began making calls.

With Hashem's help, I found some volunteers who could stay with Shira Weiner's father-in-law, and was able to greet my children properly, without the phone attached to my ear...

The excitement continued into the next day, in a different form.

"Mrs. Stein?" It was elderly Mr. Dubin, and the agitation in his voice was audible. "I'm still here at home. My ride never showed up, and I really needed that appointment. Now they're going to charge me for missing the appointment, and oh, what a mess!"

"Oh, Mr. Dubin, I'm so sorry that happened!"

"I'm so aggravated, I don't know what to do with myself!" he ranted. "I just spoke with Michael, the volunteer who was supposed to pick me up, last night, and he confirmed the time he would come. But now he's not even answering his phone!"

"Let me see if I can reach him." I tried to make my voice as calm as possible. "I'm sure there's a reasonable explanation. Maybe you can call your doctor and tell them what happened, and they can still squeeze you in—I imagine Michael will still be able to take you, if you can work that out. I'm really so sorry."

"Well, thank you for what you *tried* to do."

I just sighed.

When I called Michael, he answered the phone right away, bursting into a sincere apology. "Mrs. Stein, I feel horrible! Oh my gosh! I forgot to set my alarm clock… I just overslept… Oh, oh, oh…" He honestly sounded close to tears.

"I don't know who I feel worse for, you or Mr. Dubin," I murmured. "Look, I told Mr. Dubin to see if he can reschedule the appointment. So if you can call him and explain what happened—you're human, and you made a human error—maybe everything can still work out. Please let me know."

A few hours later, I received a call back from Michael. He sounded much better. "Mr. Dubin was able to get a later appointment. I took him, and everything worked out."

I exhaled in relief. Thank You, Hashem!

MAGNIFICENT TAPESTRY

MIRACLES HAPPEN EVERY day. Sometimes they are as brilliantly clear as the noontime sun, and other times we have to peer behind the wispy clouds, parting the curtain to see them. Not long ago, I was privileged to see yet another wreath of Bikur Cholim miracles.

A local rehabilitation facility asked me to give a staff training session in "Judaism 101" so that they could better serve their Jewish clientele. I agreed, and the night before my class, I began looking through my house and gathering some artifacts to make the presentation more lively. Rifling through the cabinets, I quickly collected a siddur, Havdalah essentials, a shofar, and a menorah.

Now where were the electric candlesticks that people use in hospitals when they're not allowed to light real candles? That would be the perfect item for this Show 'n Tell! I searched the only two places I'd ever kept them, but they weren't there. After a few more fruitless minutes of searching, I gave up the hunt and shrugged, deciding that I had better pen some notes and stop worrying about what I couldn't find.

Just as I sat down and began writing, my phone rang.

"Call from..." my phone announced, and I jumped. It was Marla—someone I couldn't ignore.

Brilliant, driven, boasting more letters behind her name than I could count, Marla had everything going for her. Employed as a professor in a reputable university, she was going places. Until she was struck down in her prime with MS. In the course of a few years, her body had degenerated to such an extent that she became an invalid.

A friend connected me with her, and I began to visit Marla regularly. After several years of visiting and forming a bond with this incredible woman, I was saddened to hear that Marla would be moving away, to sunny California, where she'd have more family support.

I hadn't spoken to Marla in months, although I often wondered how she was doing. And now, here she was, calling me!

"Marla, how are you? It's so good to hear your voice!"

We spoke for a while, and then I noticed a car pull up in front of my house. Leah Keller, a woman from the community, stepped out and began walking up my driveway, holding an unusually shaped package.

Still talking to Marla, I opened the door—and gasped when I saw what was in her hands.

"Marla, I have to go now," I said, my eyes riveted to my visitor. "Someone's at my door. It was wonderful speaking to you! You're always in our prayers."

After Marla had hung up, I ushered Leah inside.

"Rachel, I am so sorry," Leah began. "We borrowed these candlesticks from you six months ago when my father-in-law had surgery, and I kept remembering and then forgetting to bring them back. There's really no excuse for such neglect; I only hope you'll forgive me."

"Forgive you?" I laughed, my eyes dancing as I held out my hands for the candlesticks. "There's nothing to forgive. I haven't needed them all this time. But *just today*, a few minutes ago, actually, I began looking for them for a class I'm giving tomorrow. And now, just in time, here they are. Thank you *so* much!"

"You're just trying to be nice," Leah protested.

"No, I'm really not," I insisted. "It's an absolute miracle that you came now, just in time. Want to sit down?"

We shmoozed for a few minutes, and our conversation drifted to Bikur Cholim. I shared Marla's story with Leah, explaining that Marla was now living in a distant suburb of California, far away from any Jewish community.

"You don't know anyone living around those parts of California, do you? I'd love for her to have some Jewish visitors." I only threw the question out, because, well, you just never know.

"Why don't you try Chabad?" Leah suggested. "I'm pretty sure they have something over there."

I called our local branch of Chabad. The woman who answered the phone heard me out and then asked me for Marla's contact information. I wondered what would come of this.

I didn't have to wait long to find out. The very next day, I received an email from a very sweet-sounding woman in California:

Dear Rachel,

Just wanted to let you know, I had a wonderful visit with Marla yesterday. (We don't live too far from her.) What a brilliant woman! Time-permitting, my kids and I will b'ezras Hashem *continue to keep tabs on her.*

Tizki l'mitzvos,

Ariella Zelcer

I marveled at the magnificent tapestry that had been woven before my eyes. The stitches connected with amazing precision, starting with Marla's perfectly timed phone call. That was sewn to the candlesticks which appeared in Leah's hands just when I needed them. Thread that pieced together with Leah's help in getting Marla a visitor—and Hashem's handprint was unmistakable. Who else could create a picture of such majesty and genius?

PART 7
AFTERWORD

NESTLED IN MY neighborhood is a beautiful walking trail, hedged in by tall, majestic trees and lush green slopes. Beginning with a steep decline, the path curves up and down small hills, gracefully winding around a sun-drenched, glistening stream and gushing waterfall. At the very end, the trail becomes somewhat steep again, and once you reach that last part, you feel winded and exhilarated at the same time.

So has been my journey with Bikur Cholim. The patients and families I have been privileged to meet have touched my life in a deep, ineffable way, with their courage, perseverance, and often rock-like *emunah*. These people have been plunged into a world of sickness—yet their beauty shines forth, shimmering like sunbeams on a rushing stream, rushing forth like a powerful waterfall. Although their path curves and they can't see what will transpire around the bend, they continue their awe-inspiring trajectory. I feel humbled to have the opportunity to walk alongside these extraordinary individuals and to continue watching their suns rise ever higher, even as they pant to the finish line.

At the same time, I am awed by the *zechus* I have to be working with extraordinary volunteers and my devoted co-presidents and committee leaders, each of whom is an inspiration to me in his or her own right.

May Hashem bring health and healing to all of Klal Yisrael, so that the services of every *bikur cholim* organization become needless (except when it's for the joyous occasion of a baby's birth, of course!), and may all of Klal Yisrael merit to greet Mashiach together, healthy and whole, *b'meheirah b'yameinu.*

PART 8
BIKUR CHOLIM
HALACHIC APPENDIX
BY: RABBI REUVEN STEIN

*T*HERE ARE VARIOUS sources in the Torah for the mitzvah of *bikur cholim*:

1. In *Devarim* (13:5), we are told: *Acharei Hashem teilei-chu*—You should follow after Hashem. The Gemara (*Sotah* 14a) asks: How is this possible? Hashem is a consuming fire; He has unlimited power. How can humans of flesh and blood imitate that? The Gemara answers: We are commanded to follow in the *middos* of Hashem. We can "follow after Hashem" by doing those deeds that we find Hashem doing in the Torah.

   We find in the Torah that Hashem does *bikur cholim*.

In *Parshas Vayeira* (18:1), Hashem visits Avraham Avinu when he is recovering from his *bris milah*.[1] Just as we see Hashem doing *bikur cholim*, so too must we.

2. In *Vayikra* (19:18), it says, *V'ahavta l'rei'acha kamocha*— You should love your fellow as yourself. According to Rabi Akiva, this mitzvah is the fundamental rule of the Torah.

If a person isn't feeling well, needs help, or is lonely, he would certainly want others to visit him and offer assistance. Since that's what one would want for himself, he should do the same for others.

3. In *Vayikra* (19:16), it says, *Lo sa'amod al dam rei'echa*—Do not stand by while your friend's blood is being spilled. In a case where neglect to visit the sick could actually cause the patient to become worse (such as where a visitor could have noticed a problem in the patient's care and corrected it, or where a lack of visitors makes the patient become depressed, which has a negative effect on his health), the one who refrains from *bikur cholim* would be transgressing this negative commandment. In the Gemara (*Nedarim* 40a), Rabi Akiva even goes so far as to say that one who doesn't visit a sick person is compared to one who spills blood. How can that be? If the patient could have been helped, yet his health declined and he died due to purposeful neglect, the "non-visitor" would be guilty of bloodshed.

---

1 Rav Moshe Feinstein, in *Darash Moshe* (*Parshas Vayeira*, page 11), points out: The two important reasons for the mitzvah of *bikur cholim* are to help the sick person by seeing to his needs, and to pray for the sick person that he recover. Hashem did not need to visit Avraham to accomplish these goals, yet He still went to visit Avraham, *kavayachol*, when he was sick. This teaches us that even if we think we can't help the sick person, there is still a mitzvah to visit him *l'Shem Shamayim*.

The Rambam (*Hilchos Avel* 14) lists *bikur cholim* as a rabbinic mitzvah.

The *Shulchan Aruch* (3:35) codifies the laws of *bikur cholim*. The following are the basic *halachos* for this mitzvah:

1. The main fulfillment of *bikur cholim* is to evaluate and see if there's any way to help the sick person. (The word *bikur* literally means to check or to evaluate.) The Gemara (*Nedarim* 40a) mentions that Rabi Akiva went to visit a sick student and saw that he needed his room cleaned. He personally cleaned the room in fulfillment of the mitzvah of *bikur cholim*.

2. If the possibility exists that one's visit may disturb the patient, one should not go without first ascertaining if the visit would indeed be helpful or not. If one finds out that the patient is physically or emotionally not up to having visitors, one should refrain from visiting.

3. One can fulfill the mitzvah of *bikur cholim* each time he visits the patient, even if it's many times a day.

4. One should show extreme respect in the presence of a sick person, for the *Shechinah* resides there.

5. Part of the mitzvah of *bikur cholim* requires that one should pray for the sick person's recovery. When in the presence of the sick person, one can pray in any language and doesn't even need to mention the sick person's name. The Gemara (*Brachos* 34a) learns this from Moshe's *tefillah* for his sister, Miriam, when she was stricken with *tzara'as*; his prayer was simply, "*Kel na refa na lah*—Please, Hashem, heal her now" (*Bamidbar* 12:13).

6. When one is not in the presence of the sick person, one should pray for the patient in *Lashon Hakodesh*.

7. When one *davens* for a specific sick person, his prayer

should include all the other Jews in need of healing, too (i.e., one should add the words, "*besoch she'ar cholei Yisrael*—among the other sick people in Klal Yisrael").

8. If one is unable to visit a patient in person, it is still part of the mitzvah of *bikur cholim* to call on the phone and show one's concern in that way (*Igros Moshe, Yoreh De'ah,* 1:223).

9. One can do *bikur cholim* on Shabbos. Some avoid *bikur cholim* on Shabbos if doing so will make the visitor so upset that it will ruin his joy. But this, of course, should be tempered with weighing the sick person's need for a visit.

10. On Shabbos, one should not pray for and mention one's *brachah* to the sick person in the same way as he would during the week. Rather, one should say the following: "*Shabbos hi milizok u'refuah kerovah lavo*—It is Shabbos, and thus we must not cry out, but healing shall soon arrive."

11. One should consult with his *rav* regarding *bikur cholim* in the following cases: A) if one is a *kohen* and there may be a situation of *tumas meis* (spiritual defilement caused by a *kohen* coming in contact with a corpse) in the hospital where the patient resides; B) if one is a man and the sick person is a woman, or vice versa; C) if one is not on good terms with the patient; D) whether or not one is allowed to pray for a sick person's suffering to end.

REWARDS FOR *BIKUR CHOLIM*:

REGARDING SOME MITZVOS, if one benefits from them in This World, it detracts from his reward in *Olam Haba. Bikur cholim* is one of six mitzvos where, even if one benefits from them in This World, it does not take away anything from the great reward awaiting the person in *Olam Haba*. For example, many times, visiting the sick can lead to friendship and a close relationship with the patient. It can also lead the visitor to learning many important lessons about the value of life and health. But none of these benefits would detract anything from the reward the visitor will receive in the Next World for fulfilling the mitzvah of *bikur cholim*.

The Gemara (*Nedarim* 40a) says in the name of Rav that one who visits the sick will be saved from the judgment of Gehinnom. He will avoid suffering and afflictions in This World and will be able to conquer his *yetzer hara*. Many learn that this is *middah k'neged middah*, measure for measure. When one visits a sick person, he tries to help him get better and ease his suffering. He also tries to encourage him in his faith in Hashem and not let the *yetzer hara* get the better of him. *Middah k'neged middah*, Hashem will do the same for the visitor.

Additionally, if one empathizes with another's suffering, it brings him atonement, and he will not need to go to Gehinnom.